UNSILENCED

First published in 2025

www.darajapress.com
info@darajapress.com

www.horizons.com.mt
info@horizons.com.mt

© Literary rights: The authors, 2025
© Edition rights: Horizons and Daraja Press, 2025

Book production and print: Outlook Coop
Cover production: Outlook Coop

ISBN: 978-1-998309-54-2

All rights reserved. No part of this publication may be reproduced, stored in a retrieval system, or transmitted, in any form or by any means, electronic, mechanical, photocopying, recording or otherwise, without the prior consent of the authors and publishers.

Library and Archives Canada Cataloguing in Publication
Title: Unsilenced : poems for Palestine / edited by John P. Portelli.
Other titles: Unsilenced (Cantley, Quebec)
Names: Portelli, John P. (John Peter), editor
Identifiers: Canadiana 20250161028 | ISBN 9781998309542 (softcover)
Subjects: LCSH: Arab-Israeli conflict—Poetry. | LCSH: Palestinian Arabs—Poetry. | LCSH: English poetry—21st century. | LCSH: Palestine—Social conditions—Poetry. | LCGFT: Poetry.
Classification: LCC PN6110.A76 U57 2025 | DDC 821/.920803585694—dc23

UNSILENCED
POEMS FOR PALESTINE

EDITOR
JOHN P. PORTELLI

To the memory of all those killed in genocides

There is no first poet, neither a second.
There are only voices that join together and dwell together.
Life includes enough poetry for a multitude of poets
to tell their story and articulate humanity.

Mahmoud Darwish

TABLE OF CONTENTS

Introduction   15

Acknowledgments   17

Raed Anis Al-Jishi
The Eyes of Gaza   19

Ridvan Ardiç
The Revolution Will Not Be Posted on Instagram   21

Lil Blume
Trigger Warning   23

Taghrid Bou Merhi
The Flower of Cities   25

Hasan Bozdaş
A Fig for the Middle East   26

Norbert Bugeja
Kalandia   28

Tatev Chakhian
Small Talk at a Bar with a Palestinian Hunk that Would Continue through the Nights of Dresden, a City Whose memory Belongs to Neither of Us   29
One Bed, Two Wars   30

Franca Colozzo
The Knights of the Apocalypse   31
The Slaughter of the Innocents   33

Lana Derkač
Bones of Silence   34
Poem for a Refugee   35

Josie Di Sciascio-Andrews
    War Believers   36
    War on the Planet   37
    Mosque   38

Leanne Ellul
    what can i tell you about gaza   39

Mar Fenech
    Shavasana   41

Abigail George
    What It Feels Like to Be a Memory   42
    Refaat Alareer   43
    Nusayba Alareer   44
    Thirst   45

Joe Giampaolo
    Nemesis   46

Elham Hamedi
    The Glass Eyes Are Still Unbroken   47

Xanthi Hondrou-Hill
    No More Counting Stars   48
    Pray for Peace   49

Jennifer Hosein
    The Absence of Heaven   50
    All the King's Men   52

Fady Joudah
    And Out of Nowhere a Girl Receives an Ovation   53
    Mimesis   54

Rula Kahil
    Unwritten, yet Carved   55
    The Sea Holds   56
    The Architecture of Assault   57

Sheema Kalbasi
    The Children of Fig Trees and Cherry Blossoms   58
    Peace   59

Zeynep Karaca
    A Bomb Explodes on the Screen in the Rain:
    About You and Me   60

Nibal Khalil
    Homeland   62
    Childhood in Golan   63
    Exile   64
    My Orphan Country   65
    Death Portray   66

Yahia Lababidi
    Hope   67
    What to Bring to a War Protest   68
    Alternative Scenario   69
    During a Genocide   70
    Waking Nightmares   71

Milica Jeftimijević Lilić
    The Touch of a Distance   72
    The Presence of Absence   73

Sonia Maddouri
    Braids of a Jerusalemite Girl   74

Lisa Suhair Majaj
    The Burning   77
    This is a Body   78
    Ya 'Amar   80
    Shroud of Light   82
    What We Carry   84

Marwan Makhoul
    Hello Beit Hanoun   85
    New Gaza   87

The Exodus from Ireland	90
Portrait of the Family of Gaza	92
An Arab at Ben Gurion Airport	94

Leila Marshy
Exit Visa	98
Kingship	99
Where Is My Country?	100

Ahmed Miqdad
O Sea	102
Picturesque	103
Don't Count	104
If I Were	105
Where Am I from?	106

Maria Miraglia
Gaza	107

Walid Nabhan
Gaza's Golgotha	108

Mirela Necula
We Have the Right, the Right to …	109
Tuck Me in	110

Mansour Noorbakhsh,
My Journey	111

Joseph C. Ogbonna
The Israel - Gaza War	112
Mother Gaza	113

Muhammed Hüseyin Özer
Once upon a Time	114

Gianna Patriarca
Controllers	116

John P. Portelli
   You Swallow Your Anger   117
   Dreaming of Tomorrow   118
   After the Genocide   119
   Pretense   120
   Hope?   121

Niloy Rafiq
   The Bellicose   122

Shirani Rajapakse
   On the Beach   123
   Somewhere in Gaza   124
   Hope   126

Giovanna Riccio
   The Mother of All Bombs   127
   My House   128

Omar Sabbagh
   The Unimaginable   130
   Peace   131
   Christmas, 2023   132
   Lost Sundays   133

Paul Salvatori
   heartless state   134
   wrath   135
   northern migration   136

Eray Saricam
   But Were They All Naughty?   137

Zulal Sema
   Live Blog: Gaza – Non-intervention Principle   139

Cao Shui
   The Shape of the Palestinian Son   144

Kadir Tepe
    The Sweater Woven from the Thread of the
    Sirat Bridge   145

Klara Vassallo
    Running Order   147

Graciela Noemi Villaverde
    Gaza   149

Mirela Leka Xhava
    The Bell Tolls for You!   150

Anna Yin
    Winter Solstice Shades of the Name   151
    Christmas Eve   152
    Shades of the Name   153

Ghassan Zaqtan
    Oh River, Oh River   154
    Black Horses   155
    The Dead in the Garden   156

Notes on Contributors   157

INTRODUCTION

Italo Calvino wrote, "I write poetry when I have a thought that I absolutely have to bring out; I write to give vent to my feelings." The poets represented in this anthology have felt passionately and thought deeply about the situation in Gaza since October 2023, as well as the conditions in Palestine since the Nakba in 1948. They have felt morally compelled to express their emotions about the injustice inflicted on a nationless people, particularly as the tragic circumstances intensified. However, their feelings are accompanied by serious contemplation regarding the predicament that the Western world seems indifferent to, at least from those who are formally politically responsible. This has sharpened the intensity behind the more passionate and articulate calls to halt the genocide, foster compassion, and seek justice. The moral outrage expressed in these poems is rooted in the way of thinking that civilized countries and liberal democracies are supposed to honour. Unfortunately, recent history has revealed the dangers of playing a political game with double standards in the discourse concerning "the rule of law." It appears that certain international laws are not intended to be upheld by specific countries, with no repercussions to be faced.

Mahmoud Darwish, according to several literary critics, believed that poetry should allow for contemplation and that his poetry connects the daily with the ontological while simultaneously having the capacity to resist those who oppress. The poets in this collection, some of whom have directly experienced oppression – including the very oppression that Palestinians still endure – offer poetry as a means of contemplating what is, what should be, and what could be. Some of the Palestinian authors represented here have firsthand experience of the present unbearable and inhumane conditions in their homeland. Others have communicated with them and supported them in various ways, including publishing poems on social media as a form of support and resistance. Ultimately, the poems in this collection present various articulations of the relationship between the authors' feelings about daily life and their ontological stances on the human predicament. As Marwan Makhoul has brilliantly observed: "In order for me to write poetry that isn't political, I must listen to the birds, and in order to hear the birds, the warplanes must be silent." The feelings of daily life relate to the ontology of living, and ontology cannot exist in a decontextualized or neutralized setting; ontology is also intricately political. In other words, as Edward Said claimed, poetry is ultimately the personal expression of the politics of the heart!

Like Darwish, many poets in this collection turn to nature to convey their emotions of anger, disgust, and protest – sometimes in silence and pain, and other times through satire. Their imagery and metaphors reference a variety of natural objects: watermelons, carob trees, cherries, figs, birds, the sea, rivers, horses, soil, garden grass, the winter solstice, gazelles, hyenas, spiders, dogs, the relentless sun, sunsets, wind, crows, beaches, Dacian flowers, and streams. Their laments encompass homeland, childhood, exile, genocide, and war. They envision and dream of tomorrow and other possible worlds in which "the impossible is made real" (Makhoul). There is also a strong longing for peace intertwined with hope, although at times, even that hope is questioned, given the harshness of the context.

The poets included in this anthology hail from various parts of the world and have experienced diverse life journeys. However, they all agree that the actions taken against Palestine are inhumane and that these actions reveal the double standards established by the West.

In her renowned 1985 essay "Poetry Is Not a Luxury," Audre Lorde remarked: "Poetry is not a luxury. It is a vital necessity of our existence. It shapes the quality of the light through which we predicate our hopes and dreams toward survival and change, first formed into language, then into ideas, and finally into more tangible actions." In this collection, the authors act and resist through their poetry, believing it can lead to positive change.

All proceeds from the sale of this collection will be donated to Gaza.

John P. Portelli
27 January 2025
Toronto

ACKNOWLEDGMENTS

I thank all the authors who eagerly contributed to this collection. I am very grateful to all those who contributed financially to support the publication of this collection. I thank Professor Terence Portelli and AyahVictoria McKhail for their feedback. This anthology would not have been possible without the enthusiasm and support of Horizons in Malta and Daraja Press in Quebec, Canada.

RAED ANIS AL-JISHI
The Eyes of Gaza

As much as the oppression of the letters of silence
I lisped my history on the page of time

I traded until a deferred tear dried
And the gallows of ropes strutted
In the noose of silence and sounds

We own everything on our land
Even our roots were nourished by our ancestors
And grow from their decay

Even the stones that restored the pulse of our homes
Have what our heart has
From the pain of flowering

Therefore, if a child throws the stones at a castle of injustice
They increase in density of souls
And demolish the wall of illusion, falsehood and hatred

For its missile, the child of the slingshots has grown
As the old man of keys has grown far from home
but kept his heart, in the mouth of the home

We have to die now so that we can increase
The thickness of the earth's dignity and majesty.

And to light the dark world with torches
for every martyr whose ribs have exploded
from the bombing and torture
perceived a fire.
And returned to light the path from the Heart of a burning ember

Lonely since it was torn and bent
The remains of the burning ember walk in the form of a revolution

Death cannot be silent, and perhaps
(Palestine) before death was written
On the clay tablet of fate in the depths of a firing hole

And it was not miswritten, but the passion wanted it
To be contained in the eye of "Gaza"

RIDVAN ARDIÇ
The Revolution Will Not Be Posted on Instagram

I guess everything is a little nuclear,
Only one flower remains burdened with grief.
Let it grow – we'll find kingdoms to carry us,
We'll raise the apocalypse, building homes from stones,
Stretch our consciences – what harm in trying once?
Our names, a backup for everything that deceived us.

As a tank's ache stabs through Ramallah,
And the last bomb tempts us into ruin,
Our first sorrow lodges deep in rage.
Not because we settled down –
Don't forget.

33,000 killed, a few tanks exploded,
Everything – everything – a radioactive mandala.
Don't forget – one last flower still left to mourn.
If glass pierces eyes, if black swans choke in a strait,
These days' unspoken verses will be the age of daggers,
Ringing eternally in the universe's relentless cycle.
Democracy's final bomb equals nothing
But vaporizing in a wretched density.

The earth has no guest room, no place to hide.
Tell me about Bolivia's natural wonders,
Tell me about Zionism's future projections,
Tell me about the truth you harvest while separating wheat from chaff,
About the insights spun from your lies and fabricated instincts,
About the imbalance in your contrast as you bastardize every belief.
Tell me about the dissonance of living,
The voice inside you screaming OH, COME ON!

But wow, what an unnecessary use of emojis.
It didn't concern you, and how beautifully you blocked me.
You deserved to vanish in vapor – don't come near me.
You resurrected in a sturdy reel, a spirit in Sierra Maestra.

Don't forget – one last flower remains, one last bomb.
Death has taken its place in history
As a question no synthetic mind can answer.

One last scratch – this really was the last.
And I, the final one.
Carbon taxes streamed from my eyes.
Forget, if you want, the horses that escaped the film set,
Or the brats who kill without thought,
Stampeding toward you, unshod, unmasked.
But don't say you'll free me, my love –
Slavery was abolished on Instagram long ago.

LIL BLUME
Trigger Warning

*To the woman who came to the door asking that we take down our
"End the Occupation/Free Palestine" sign because she was triggered.*

Warning: This poem might trigger you.
Because when I say "Free Palestine"
You hear "Kill the Jews"
Because when I say "Nakba"
You hear "Kristallnacht"
Because when I say "Stop the genocide"
You hear "Support Hamas"

Because my sympathy for Gazans makes you uncomfortable
Because you think being uncomfortable is the same as being in danger.

Warning: The keffiyeh that this poem is wrapped in might trigger you
Might make you uncomfortable
Because when the poem sees children in Gaza burning
You only see Jewish children burning
Because this keffiyeh asks you to be aware of others, to care about others.

Warning: This poem might trigger you
Because you believe the conflict started October 7
Because you *know* your army is the most moral
Because you see genocide as self-defense
    (And, besides, the only genocide ever was the genocide of your
    people, yes, my people!)
And you'd rather not have your convictions challenged.

Because you planted a tree in Israel every Tu B'shvat
Because you didn't know the trees were planted to hide bulldozed
Palestinian villages
Because you knew it was *your* land given to you by the British, the UN,
and God
Even though it was never theirs to give.

This poem might trigger you
Because you want two million Gazans to disappear and killing them
one by one
Is too slow –
And makes you
Uncomfortable.

TAGHRID BOU MERHI
The Flower of Cities

Poetry is like living in Gaza –
No child returns twice to their mother.
Alumad Bakhit

The night draws its clouds in the darkness,
Refusing to shine within its shadow.

The wind violently storms the homes,
And the roses kneel, betrayed by those who failed them.

Patience cloaks the people like armor,
Facing injustice too cruel to bear.

Hunger gnaws at hearts, and their famine
Is pain upon pain, exile upon exile.

Yet always, our resolve exceeds our wounds,
Even as death marches forth to gather its prey.

We live, carrying in our chests a trust –
Never to walk the paths of deception.

O Gaza of the free, O cradle of sacrifice,
We will keep writing our blood upon its shores.

A thousand proud children still remain,
Stepping toward victory with unwavering resolve.

The land bears witness, and the Almighty blesses
Every steadfast heart upon this path.

So, remain strong, you who have seen our perseverance,
The resilience of the brave who would die for you.

O flower of the beautiful cities,
We offer you the love of our hearts – our greatest dream.

HASAN BOZDAŞ
A Fig for the Middle East

When I loved you, Israel did not exist
Fairuz's song
struggled to cross the wooden bridge at the border,
they could not find in it
the fear of agarwood
nor the permit granted to songs.
I shared an occupation with you
I never understood why the Nile did not drown
some were wicked, yet they loved, stitched it into a flag
they gave one dead to another, gifted to the grave
law is dead, Geneva is dead, diplomas are dead,
houses are dead, people are dead
they came, full of love.
Our garden becomes Ramallah,
and twenty kinds of figs
prophets have eaten what could grow there
then, you know, some were hanged, some were slain
only God's patience could endure it
but we have already died, and it doesn't matter much
who the wolves now feed
from tangerines that never ripen.
Tibetan horses could run
as high as six thousand meters in war
but we had no such horses, no such friends
Ghassan was killed by a bomb
Mourid by sorrow
if they cannot kill a poet with a suicide,
they will kill him with cancer anyway
I am not trembling – I think I am frozen
but the conventions tremble, humanitarian law and Oslo,
someone once said in Oslo:
"children here do not cry, only Middle Eastern ones do."
Yes, yes, exactly –
the voices of Middle Eastern children are here.

When an occupation begins, let's start with the cliché
a few black flies that think I deserve to die
a door, a key, a Shin Bet,
all waiting for me to comply.
How many capitals, how many shrines
just to meet you once again?
You know – whether or not they share the Pope's faith,
there are churches bound to fall.
Yet silence remains an option,
for global flavors are far more palatable.
Will your country believe in my skin, my tongue?
Will your country believe that I am human?
I know – babies were once sweet, but not anymore.
Bombs fall like popping corn,
rubble becomes a chamber of fear.
They think I will resurrect in the corner
the moment I die,
but it is they who live in a simulation room.
A child drowns in a grave – painful.
He left hungry – painful for his mother.
A scratch could hurt me, but they won't believe it.
I never buy cushions or glasses for my home.
I don't want them to get used to me.
Remember each home,
remember an identity in exile.
But when I went to the poet's Palestine,
I saw – tears are always close to the eye.
some flowers bloom only in death,
not red – blood.
A pacifier, a penny, a little blood.
A loaf of bread, a cat, a little blood.
A bit of tooth, a bit of dream, a little blood.
long enough for a dream,
but I do not want,
I do not want to be dead forever –
or a figurine of a man.

Translated by Kadir Tepe

NORBERT BUGEJA
Kalandia

Night weighs heavily on the checkpoint at Kalandia,
pregnant with this foetus pushing inwards
like half a lemon bobbing in a cup –
craving a spot closer to the heart.
Is it the stars that are drifting, she asks,
or have the clouds suddenly stood still?
The mind grows foggy at Kalandia,
troubles the officer's thoughts
as they linger over Noura's belly
nursing her silent wound over the fence.
This young man studied philosophy,
knows by heart the history of his exile
and Arendt's writings on how twilight, too,
will learn to live on the edges.
Words smudge beneath Noura's gaze,
the child keeps pushing until its head bends –
key to no door, key without a lock
but for the fatiha before sunset,
the distant echo of *samba de janeiro*.
Closer to the heart, her kohl drips
and drowns the lemon in the soldier's cup.

Translated from the Maltese by Irene Mangion

TATEV CHAKHIAN
Small Talk at a Bar with a Palestinian Hunk that Would Continue through the Nights of Dresden, a City Whose memory Belongs to Neither of Us

— As children, we're ashamed to speak of defeat.
— As we grow older, we don't know how to bear it.
— Defeat is a cancer; you cure it by killing.
— The winner gets his dream, the beaten – what's left.
— That much? he wonders.
— That little, I confess.
— Come closer, he whispers.

Translated from Armenian by the author

One Bed, Two Wars

In someone else's homeland,
on someone else's New Year's Eve,
beneath someone else's shuddering sky,
our bodies crumble to dust.

We share one bed and two wars.

He fears that death
might stretch longer than life.
I soothe him – once you get used to it, the pain dulls.
History books call it *resilience* –
a noble folk garment on a filthy body.
It stinks, but at least it's warm.
You ain't cold, are you?

In someone else's homeland,
on someone else's New Year's Eve,
beneath someone else's shuddering sky,
the streets are stuffed with ground meat.
Sulfur thickens the air,
noise swells – a howl tongueless and faceless.

I shut the window.
We lie down in silence.
Silent – like a house
where the TV is left on,
but no one's home.

Translated from Armenian by the author

FRANCA COLOZZO
The Knights of the Apocalypse

Four Knights come at a trot
They sow hatred, they are Black Ravens.
They pay the price of a recent past,
They raise shields that imprison our mind
Sad for the dead in the Holocaust.

Even my father follows
The procession of the living dead,
He knows the hell of the Nazi camps,
He knows captivity and torturers.
Escaped yesterday, he died before time ...

Shadows walk now,
the night lengthens ...
The waning crescent moon
everything discolors,
everything overshadows,
amid chaos and prayers, missiles and bombs,
everything spreads like wildfire.
But what are the children to blame
If Palestine is only weeping?
Seeds and roots kneaded with hatred
Land abused, violated, stolen,
misallocated by those who make History.

Hitler smiles, a greedy ghost
Blood and memories, sewn up to harm,
Judge God yields to deception,
comes to his impostor sons
Who from the Holy Book
New prisons have basted.

What Messiah can ever come
Perhaps to finish the horrid havoc?
Loudly implored
From the Wailing Wall, now hides himself
Behind foreign wings.

Mute is Hell! Shots of bombs,
blood and perjury,
A unicorn rises in the sky
But there is a dragon advancing
Swift through fire and flame.
The mendacious man followed Cain,
mourns the woman who begat him,
evil son produces outrage.

The Slaughter of the Innocents

Wings spread to the wind, they rise
In a silent procession,
Drifting like feathers,
They ascend into flight
From the hospital in Gaza,
Struck to the ground by a missile,
Tearing through its ancient heart.

They all rise together like Seraphim
Stolen from the games of another time.
The game of massacre now knows no end.
Crow's wings fly over the ruins,
Brushing against angel wings in the sky.

The evening turns pale
Amidst ghostly figures.
Only the rubble mourns the dead,
Dead without a true reason,
A common burial remains
For scattered limbs.

The children are no longer afraid,
The hellish roars fall silent,
Hunger and thirst fall silent.
Their creations are offered to God
By grieving mothers as a gift.
From the altars of light, a dark image,
A sacrilegious land reveals
The infamous offspring of Cain.

LANA DERKAČ
Bones of Silence

Even silence has bones.

I wonder what kind of sound they make
and how much rheumatism they can attract.

When I stumble upon a mass grave
walking in a field
I praise the benevolence of birds
who wrap up the bones they find
with their song
as if providing them with new tissue.

Translated by Damir Šodan

Poem for a Refugee

Every island is a scar on water.
Stars are open wounds on darkness.
The terrace I'm sitting on is too far
to throw Tyrosur to any of them –
the powder against infections.

Each refugee is an island. Rifat is an island as well. Layal too.
So what if the island moves!
If it glides across water, grass, asphalt only to end up stranded
against a mountain, an army or a wire?

He is a man-rock, he could just as well have been a woman-rock
as the border police comb the meadow with refugee-rocks
like they're going through drawers.
Rifat stares at the screen of the horizon as if it's a TV-set,
hearing the thunder like it's the most powerful sound ever.
The field where he is sitting in is his living room, his kitchen,
even his shower cabin for the clouds are pissing down on him.
They have already taken it too far this time.

In the morning a lame cloud is filling a samovar at the antiques fair.
Not sensing that the next one will wet the medallion
on the stand, that once belonged to Rifat.
Or that a fly will easily fly over the fur coat,
the border preventing the medallion from reaching the western end
    of the table.

Every island is a scar on the smooth surface.
Stars are wounds on darkness.
My terrace is too far for the celestial hand to reach
the bottle with Tyrosur. Sparing itself from an infection.

Translated by Damir Šodan

JOSIE DI SCIASCIO-ANDREWS
War Believers

These are the ones
That would hesitate
At the thought of ending wars,
As if you were taking away
Their right to breathe.

"What? No killing?
It's what we live for.
The essence of a man."

These are the ones
Who swear
By honour
Righteousness.

These are the ones
Who obey
Rules and rulers;
Who stick to truths
As sharp as blades,
Passions as red
As homicide.

War on the Planet

At this very moment,
Someone is dying.
Another Christ
Is staggering in a city alley
Or behind a barbed wire wall,
In a desert
To his own Golgotha,
That ever-present place of skulls.
Random is this death,
Multiplied to the 'nth power of blood
Under the light of a relentless sun.

At this very moment,
A child is being born.
Bundles of hope
Swaddled in innocence while
With their strategic plans and war scrolls,
Corporations and heads of state
Wait to harvest him away
From his crib of dreams and lullabies.

At this very moment,
A poet is writing
Of men dying,
Of children hatching in mine fields,
While scornful
The powerful plot their ploys of gain
Unaffected by poems or human tears.

Mosque

We escaped into the sweltering darkness of an alley. Footsteps of armed soldiers echoed on the humid cobblestones, feverishly reflecting the illumination of the mosque beyond the rooftops. The light led us to the monolith. From mullioned windows, telescopes scanned the city. High-tech devices with weapon capabilities. We hid from their beams into a shadowed stairway down to the riverbank. In the twilight, we witnessed people being carried off by the current, children waving their arms, drowning. And an old oracle slumped by the edge, watching.
It happens every day now. He cried dolefully. *It's the end of times.*

LEANNE ELLUL
what can I tell you about gaza?

I've no clue like children's blabber
without   a tongue
running   from somewhere to nowhere
        like a scattering
from where to begin
            when your city is on fire
when here we only know of fiery summers
                    how to sweat blood
the bombs' fir   how it burns
the morsels   of days
I remember telling you war immobilises me
     do you remember   how
I was telling you about the war   once
and gaza   **what can I tell you about gaza?**   that
we were born during a war that's ongoing
somewhere else   and while it grew with us
    we still don't know what it is   and we don't even know
            if we care
how sometimes we try to grasp an end and find ends
      what is happening   there   the blood
            of the world   what are
sumac   saffron   maqluba
taboon   maftoul
they seem like ours   but   they're not
seems like land but it's not
seems like a game   a buried   ball
what can I tell you?
that it's not palestine
     but also   right
we hear   we lose   our breath
just imagine
assuming that if you don't see   t is not there
like fine salt   like melted sugar
you know how   a question already answered
the punctuation's not necessary

like   a war that doesn't know about periods
there are children who don't even know a dummy
what can I tell you about gaza?   how many
mass ridicules
on silver plates
nations torn from their land
lines of castrated chalk
like pulling a plaster
                    and at the same time swearing
I don't know   how   to put conscience to sleep
much faster   than putting a baby to sleep
          what can I tell you about gaza?
how my hand searches for it on a map
this story of a story   at night
trucks track along the edge of path   they do
the remains remain   **what can I tell you about gaza?**
why a strip   not a band
I think it suits it more
don't you think   I search for the etymology of
conflict not where conflict began
where it came from   how it started   the word
the war   isn't easy to understand
this isn't like war

*An English reworking of the poem "x'naqbad ngħidlek fuq gaza?" written originally in Maltese (**Il-Ħsad tal-Peprin**, Horizons, 2024).*

MARTHESE FENECH
Shavasana

And how can the light in me
Honour the light in you
When my light burns so dim
Because I can't hold
Downward dog for fifteen seconds
Without thinking about the
Fifteen children
Who have lost limbs and lives to rockets
In the time it takes me to get the pose
Right
Or when I stand in Vrksasana and stretch my arms
Like branches to the sky
I do not see the stars
Only a constellation of scars
And I think of all the olive trees
Uprooted like so many lives
And child's pose
How do I rest in child's pose
When
New phrases have been born to describe
A wounded child with no surviving family
And tin foil serves as an incubator
How do I breathe a deep Ujjayi breath
When the generator has just run out and the
Oxygen stops and that final gasp
And
Shavasana.

ABIGAIL GEORGE
What It Feels Like to Be a Memory

The whole of Palestine has turned into a sea.
The sea is just another dead poet. Just another
martyr.
The sea knows death and speaks its
        language fluently,
for death has now become its mother-tongue.
Each wave has turned the graveyard over.
Bodies and the skeletons of children, the
skulls of birds, kittens and dogs have spilled
out of coffins. Who wants to think of their nearest
Macdonald's in war, getting hamburgers in war?
The Biden-administration? Blinken?
What happened to every wave in that sea, you
        just might ask?
They turned into dead poets and their words.
But wait, I am repeating myself. But didn't
you know that in the blink of an eye, one ghost
can haunt you, and a nation can disappear
without a trace, whole countries, whole
open-air prisons, and children too. This is what it
feels like to be a memory. Just an empty shell
casing, an airstrike, bombs falling, pouring
down like rain. Smoke, rubble and the dead.
In war, even the dead remember. They have a
memory, too, while the living struggle to just
survive apartheid in a brave new world.

Refaat Alareer

There is hope born in death, and death born in hope
These are not empty words, you said
I looked at the exhaustion on your face
I thought of the flowers in Gaza, the orange
and lemon trees, the last olive you ate,
the last shower you took, the last prayer
you said, the last time you boiled a
manifesto in the kettle, stirred coffee
and sugar into a mug, the last time you watched
an American film, the last newspaper you
read, the last dead body you saw, the
last book you opened, the last time you
saw your family, your wife and children.
I have stopped watching the updates of
the Palestinian genocide. They used to
call it the Palestinian-Israeli conflict, but now
it is a genocide. It's become too much
for me to take. My tears can fill an ocean
and carry the orphans in an ark until
this war is over, but there's no end to a war
like this. Perhaps when we reach the end
of the world, the war will end. Perhaps. Perhaps.

Nusayba Alareer

You were a witness to a heinous
atrocity of war, a crime against humanity
Wildflowers in open spaces
wildflowers in closed spaces
in spaces that have been tampered with
You lost a husband, your children
lost a father, the world lost a poet
I sit in my room and write this poem
I, too, am a witness of crimes against
humanity.

You, Palestine, come to me in a dream
You, Gaza, Rafah, every slain poet, every dead child
every monster in war, in life
you, every martyr, come to me
You all come to me
like Hemingway or church
like banana fish
like Fitzgerald, J.D. Salinger
John Updike
M. Night Shyamalan's
over productive imagination

Before I wake up completely
I find that I am losing my voice
that another Palestinian child
is dead (the body found in a
ditch) that there are more martyrs
today than there were yesterday
Where are all the poets and writers
Ask Refaat Alareer, he knows
Ask Omar Abu Shaweesh, he knows
Ask Yousef Dawas, he knows
How painful it is to die young
Even more painful to live with no hope,
to live with no bread, to chase
famine, to survive on dust that's
to be found in a refugee camp.

Thirst

Yehuda Amichai
Marina Tsvetaeva
Nadine Gordimer
Han Kang
Aleksandr Solzhenitsyn

Remember these names

Nadia Davids
Mongane Serote
Khaled Juma
Refaat Alareer

Although there are too many to mention
please, please, I beg you
to remember them

If you have the time
Write these names down
Study what they have to say
They are writing for the future

JOE GIAMPAOLO
Nemesis

Some say that the nemesis of fascism is democracy,
others claim its enemy is socialism.

The real enemy is art:
Freedom, truth and beauty.

Where there is art,
Fascism cannot breathe.

ELHAM HAMEDI
The Glass Eyes Are Still Unbroken

What plays within your eyes
Is the reflection of a world
That began this cruel game
Upon the field of your gaze.

What plays within your eyes
Is not a longing tear
Nestled in the glassy stare of a doll.

What plays within your eyes
Is a drop of sorrow
That makes your soul salty.

Do not close your eyes,
For the world lives in the whiteness of your eyes.

Do not close your eyes,
The doll's glass eyes remain unbroken,
And the dream of a child
Still lingers in your waking sight.

XANTHI HANDROU-HILL
No More Counting Stars

The lights are bright in Gaza
They are falling from the sky
No one is asking why
The world is home and watching
Nobody is standing by.

The lights are low in Gaza
The children went to sleep
The fathers counting bodies
The mothers will only weep.

The light's gone out in Gaza
Just poets sit and cry
For no child will ever
Look up to the night sky.

We want the children playing
out in the streets at night
No more fighting wars
We want them counting stars.

The lights gone out in Gaza
The children joined the stars
And writing on the night sky
A chant of ancient chants

NO MORE WARS!

Pray for Peace

The words of love under the trees are peace.
Giannis Ritsos

Pray for Peace
pray for your father to return in the evening
with a smile in his eyes and a basket filled with fruits.

Pray for Peace
may the wounds of the world be healed
to plant trees again where the bombs left open wounds.

Pray for Peace
so that the noise in the sky is just thunder
and the storm will bring rain to water our hopes.

Praying for Peace,
the warm food on the table of the globe,
every mother's smile at the playgrounds...

Pray for Peace,
pray for that party in the backyard,
where the children will smile in the sunset.

JENNIFER HOSEIN
The Absence of Heaven

away from home
time meanders beyond the
glimmer of Christmas lights
through rain that won't stop
on the eve of 2024

neighbours have hung
flashy balloons and rainbow flags
but the night is muted:
our bellies full
the baby settled on our laps

days pass and
in a frenzy of diapers
the baby beams and giggles so
I only think of bottles
nipples and dinner

but one evening
I open Instagram
where mothers bend over
the silence of children
waiting to be wrapped in cloth
gifts to the absence of heaven

I tug on the howl
that shoots out of me
swallowing it whole
so as not to wake the house
in the presence of this
UNIMAGINABLE

and in the morning, soothe
my grandson's hair
keening inside, though
my face is stoic and smiling
in the comfort of our heated rooms

on the last night, I break
the dishwasher in the Airbnb
ignoring the rumble inside
the bargain basement appliance
had I only listened

but I did not, and
why are we not listening:
to a world hurting
so badly it would slaughter
its children

All the King's Men

press the pause button
that is your privilege
to lean into the city lit up

like Independence Day
to fall into emancipation
and the crack of concrete, but

how can you choose this?
when those who lie beneath rubble
wait for the sky

I stay myself
against the dread of night
wind my wings around

this wound we call world
hold out my hands to pluck bits
of children from the sky: a limb

a finger, a shredded *visage*
but the kings and all the kings' men
will not put them back together again

and bombs light up the evening
like fireworks
the night of the famous gala

FADY JOUDAH
And out of nowhere a girl receives an ovation
from her rescuers,
all men
on their knees and bellies,
clearing the man-made rubble
with their bare hands,
disfigured by dust
into ghosts.
All disasters are natural,
including this one,
because humans are natural.
The rescuers tell her
she's incredible, powerful,
and for a split second, before the weight
of her family's disappearance
sinks her, she smiles
like a child
who lived for seven years above ground
receiving praise.

*Note: the original poem has no title, first published in [...],
Minneapolis, MN: Milkweed, 2024.*

Mimesis

My daughter wouldn't hurt a spider
That had nested
Between her bicycle handles
For two weeks
She waited
Until it left of its own accord

If you tear down the web I said
It will simply know
This isn't a place to call home
And you'd get to go biking

She said that's how others
Become refugees, isn't it?

*Originally published in **Alight**, Port Townsend, WA: Copper Canyon Press, 2013.*

RULA KAHIL
Unwritten, yet Carved

I was asked to write you in poetry
and unlike you, the mobilized
outside your will
outside your body land
my fingers are immobilized

Stuck. Useless. Paralyzed
unable to pick you up
stone by stone
piece by piece

My fingers are stiff
can't write you under the rubble
can't pull you out
can't decipher your pain
can't fathom the horrors

My fingers are frozen
I write you on my body
engrave you into my skin
I tattoo you.

The Sea Holds

They said it is over

You must yearn for the sea
you must yearn to gather the tears
not yet spilled
still hidden
trapped behind the horror
of the unimaginable

You yearn for the sea
in hope it can fill
the hollowness in your body
emptied by each soul that left

You yearn for the sea
to mend the wounds
your loved ones
asked you to hold on to
to never forget

They said it is over

So, you walk to the sea.

The Architecture of Assault

Haunting phrases
smudged in the love of humanity
preserving innocence for the wicked
as bloody words drip with honey

Assault – when you claim my land as yours
coated in your 'right' to share
without being invited

Assault – when your presence
is as sticky as
your claim to rights earned by me

Assault – when your humanity
Is hinged on stripping me of mine

Assault – when your love is a bargain
an exchange of every drop of my being

Assault – when you pose as the righteous victim
ignoring the violent interplay
between your world and mine

Assault –
and you   the master of it.

SHEEMA KALBASI
The Children of Fig Trees and Cherry Blossoms

The children, fig-fed and cherry-cheeked,
Whip through the shoreline's sandy strip,
Their laughter a brittle thread.
They pile the rocks, bones of the shore,
Shape their castles with salt-stung hands.
They uncover what scripts they find
Are not their own –
The letters bruise like fingerprints,
Secrets clawing up through packed sands.
Winter arrives with its axe –
The fig trees split; the blossoms spill.
The castles crumble to brittle dust.
Graves small as birthdays line the frozen earth,
Clapboard markers for lives unspoken.
A mother's body beneath the bed,
A father smears into the walls,
Time's cruel varnish.
A dog paces, pacing, pacing,
Waiting endlessly at the gate.
Skulls settle –
Unharvested, unloved,
Noiseless, nameless,
Familyless, friendless, forgotten.

Peace

Let us write about peace,
Of pain hidden within the PEACE.
When Hindus and Sikhs were forced to roam
From their homes on Punjab's soil, for mercy's sake.
Of struggles in days of old,
The native souls and their lands beset,
Cherokee, Muscogee, Seminole's grace,
Chickasaw and Choctaw's sacred place.
Let us write about the PAIN.

Let us, piece by piece, write about the peace,
Much like a piece of meat
Or an incomplete puzzle to trace,
Bearing witness to massacres by the side of the roads.

Let us, piece by piece, write about a peace,
With quill or pen,
Of the vision for paradise and peace.

Slice and cut,
Sow,
Sow,
The fragile piece of flesh, pin it to the chest,
Piece by piece,
When zombies intoxicated by ideology ascend,
To dismember, piece by piece.

ZEYNEP KARACA
A Bomb Explodes on the Screen in the Rain: About You and Me

it rained all day
the ground is wet, the sky is wet, everything in between is wet
somewhere, the sound of a bomb
I see it on Twitter, it pops up in reels
bombs drop often on YouTube, too
but I just stand here, loving you
I have a window – you'd like it if you knew it
so open, so full of the world, so full of people
if you touched the glass, you'd understand
sometimes, I want to be grass
to feel the rain better
I want to be a tree too
to crave the earth more
I tell myself I should be the sky
bringing you clouds, endlessly
steep roads, walking, and a bit of you
these things feel good, like dreams of tobacco and good bread
time rushes by at my computer
I open your photo, full-screen
it feels like I've brought you home
somewhere, bombs explode
children die smiling at their mothers
we look ahead, thankful to be alive
children die too much, in front of screens
I weave a tangled dream, about you and me
somewhere, a child takes revenge on life
with a stone and a slingshot
I wake as if from a dream
it rains, about you and me

someone must have made gains today –
on the stock market, in gold, in dollars
someone must have had fine wine
spent the evening in an expensive restaurant
stacked wealth upon wealth;

and here I am, at my window,
with the sound exploding in my head
the most beautiful dreams of you:
is humanity vile, or above all
is the earth a mystery, a reckless adventure
or will hands soon reach each other?

the water at my bedside when I wake,
the bird singing in the garden,
what is this window, open to which sky
what is this bomb, enemy to which eye
amid the rush of the world?

a little of you, a little of me
a wild daisy, off on a journey
the earth will be a beautiful, good place
believe in this poem.

Translated by Kadir Tepe

NIBAL KHALIL
Homeland

Oh, my hollow homeland sitting on your thrones
your cities passed from here
you had the scent of the soil
your sea was a rumor; its bluish exhaled up to the sky

Oh, homeland!

You hold the vineyards that bear no names
and the shadow of your mountains remained in solitude
our souls vaporized under your sun
we ambushed our lives in you.

Childhood in Golan

The stones of the alley are wrapped with silence
a song for Dalida is looming in my head
Helwah ya Baladi

I carry all the names over the burden of my rips
and time is a rope wrapped around my cold neck,
something is speaking to me,
tingling my icy hand

Every morning,
I brace myself to live like my roving childhood in the Golan
I have no duel in this battle ground except my soul
and the soul is a blanched voice in the twilight of the silence.

Exile

I am out of nothingness
I lost myself under a carob tree,
the memory box will be buried
when the first stone is placed in the cemetery.
no one will be allowed to get closer,
this is how my exile looks
ghastly
and deepened in pain.

My Orphan Country

My orphan country,
Living in the Refuge.

Today, I ordered from a tailor a needle to fix the patches of sadness on our bodies,
He told me the needle got lost under the rubble.

I asked the hairdresser for a brush to comb destruction of my country,
He said an old woman borrowed it before she died, so it went with her.

My country's face is covered with the dust of broken concrete.
So, I went to the herbalist to buy a cure for oppression,
He said he is out of the recipe.

All the women bought it to give birth to men over the graves of their fathers.

And I asked for a perfume I can smell whenever I'm unconscious,
He said it is all in the bags buried in the cemetery.

The country is an orphan, my daughter,
Wear your black forever.

Death Portrait

We hang our children by a rope on the wall of the sky,
A family portrait snapped before their dispatch.
It is crucial, you see,
That the fragments gather in a single bag...

A luxury,
To have the bag hold one whole body.
And if the world becomes too tight for us...
One bag for the whole family on the stage will suffice...
Enough for the photographer to capture his shot,
Waiting patiently
For everyone to take their turn.
"No thousand joys to come
Could ever erase this image..."

YAHIA LABABIDI
Hope

Hope's not quite as it seems,
it's slimmer than you'd think
and less steady on its feet.

Sometimes, it's out of breath
can hardly see ahead
and cries itself to sleep.

It may not tell you all this
or the times it cheated death
but, if you knew it, you'd know

how Hope can keep a secret.

What to Bring to a War Protest

Bring a candle
burning in your eyes
to lead the way,

bring a bird
nestled in your heart
to set others free

bring a shroud
large enough to bury
the dead past

bring a flag
spotless and white
to surrender pain.

Alternative Scenario

After the horrors of October 7
the good people of Palestine rushed
to the sides of stricken Israelis

Tending to the wounded,
mourning the dead,
comforting survivors

They kept vigil, praying & weeping,
delivering truckloads of flowers
serving trays, by day, of warm meals & sweets

Palestinian families flooded the streets
en masse, protesting: *Not in our Names*
demanding the return of hostages

Recognizing the great need, they gifted
what they, too, longed for: mercy, solace, solidarity –
and the world, witnessing, never forgot...

Helpless, Hamas eventually surrendered,
the Israeli government, in turn, relented
and walls in hearts crumbled, then tumbled.

During a Genocide

You will find that during a genocide,
most words lose their meaning –
some sound empty & others strange

Apart from unceasing prayer,
eloquence takes the form
of tears or kindness and solidarity

Even a quiet moan or sighing
is preferable to false words or worse:
a loud and wounding Silence...

Waking Nightmares

How is it that
life carries on,
as they cry for us,
from under the rubble?

While doctors amputate
limbs without anesthesia,
how did we staunch the wounds
of our own throbbing hearts?

The watermelons are rotten
– cut open and bone dry –
from bleeding in the streets

Watered tears, I shudder to imagine
the future of these sad seeds,
what terrible fruit will grow...

MILICA JEFTIMIJEVIĆ LILIĆ
The Touch of a Distance

My clairvoyant hands,
as hot as a sorcerer's hands
set in motion by thought
touch the chosen thing,
it is them that have encountered you.
Seeing better than the eyes
they impeccably guide me,
Logos always appeals to me.

I write down a word or two
and the rainbow gives a flash
fusing two violent waters
aware of the might of the said.
It shoots them through to the bottom
integrated by the force of origins.
Out of the overheated core
sterling flows over
with a deep trail.

I touch letters one by one,
they spread energy with ease.
Receiving it, you light up –
you open all doors
to me – a woman.
And you do not know what breaks you:
either the touch of fire or the might of the said
that defeated you at once.
Or the secret of the being from afar
that flashes when fusing with you.

Translated by Lazar Macura

The Presence of Absence

You are a black Moon that pulls me up
And I, enchanted, am climbing,
You are too present in the absence
We become one through your logos.
I am Lilith, always demanding.
You can come into me only through mind
You know that, and wait for my command.

The door of my inner self is high.
Only by a torch of words you can enter
Into the midst of the lucidity
That agitates my blood,
That embodies the river between us
To wash away our karma
Unseparated in the eternity of a poem,
To hide the midnight sun
That radiates intoxicating, but resisting.

As a black dove, I restlessly
Circle above you, suppress the pain,
Sweetly coo to call you
On the moonlight feast where I will dance
In white, like a dervish, my vertiginous dance.
When you turn ready for all,
I will disappear.

Translated by Denisa Kondić

SONIA MADDOURI
Braids of a Jerusalemite Girl

The birds pecking the heads of the Bereaved
So that the olive trees may bloom
On the lips of the trigger...
In Jerusalem, we turned our hearts towards her
Our prayer is a mother
Wiping away a tear as she cries out:
"O God, take my eyes, but leave
My son's shirt behind –
It grants me vision in his absence."

From the silver threads of forgetfulness,
She mends her wounds,
And embraces the elusive, cruel hope.

This absence is cloaked in her soul,
Entangled in the salt
Of wounded bodies...

The lovers of this land
Suddenly turned away,
Selling their honor to villains.

Once, they stood here –
Like promised seasons
Of wheat and olives,
With every harvest.

They abandoned the cities,
Leaving no solace for their orphaned memories
But the cooing of a dove on festive days.

They wander lost,
Guided only by the fire's
Hidden embers.

Their names are noble,
And every map
Is a Jerusalem fluttering
From scattered ashes.

That young traveler
Found a cloud,
Erecting tents for it
Without stakes.

From the first wind that passed,
The tears of the cloud
Spilled into the distance.

Desires surrendered to him,
He peeled away his silence,
Split longing in two,
Stained with darkness.

He wrote poems
With the blood of his eyes,
Cutting off visions
While swords remained in their sheaths.

As if the shores of exile
– All of them –
Were tides
That celebrate my ink.

The auction has begun –
A little girl:
"How much is she worth?"
"The pride of Arab glory," they say.

They bound her hands,
Her dreams,
With their iron chains,
Not knowing the eloquence of shackles.

She, who once suppressed
A child's simple wishes –
To play, to soar, to sing...

Within the belly of this whale,
Our only solace remains:
That we have sown the dream
For eternity.

A day will come
When our Jerusalem walks freely,
And all mourning will fade away.

LISA SUHAIR MAJAJ
The Burning

When will enough be enough? Aaron Bushnell walked
toward his death with a firm step, calling for freedom
for others, understanding what he was about to do
and why, aware that desperation belongs to everyone,
that we share complicity with death hurled from the sky
or scorching a sniper's gun chamber, flames swallowing
those trapped, incinerating homes and families, the fire
of hunger blazing within, denial of water turning lives
to tinder, quick to spark, till young and old are burnt
utterly, flesh sinking into ashen pallor, bones crumbling,
lives destroyed like the land, the crops, the buildings,
the fishing vessels fired on to prevent access to any food
anywhere, the ones shot while crawling across a broken
landscape toward a sack of flour so that the quest for bread
becomes a death sentence and the plea for reprieve
roars like flames in a dry forest, spreading like wildfire
across screens and airwaves till no one can claim
to be unaware of this deepening anguish, and so perhaps
it should not be a surprise when someone who sees clearly
anoints himself with gasoline, sets himself alight like a torch,
seeking to bring clarity to a world willing to burn everyone
and everything without mercy, someone who demands we face
the questions we avoid at our peril: What price destruction?
What price humanity? What price freedom? What price life?
And what will we do when the burning reaches us?

This is a Body

This is a body.
Body of flesh. Body of bone.
Body of spirit. Body of light.
Body of longing. Body of dreams.
Body of bodies.

This is a body.
Body with a chest broken open.
Body with a skull broken open.
Body with a spirit broken open.
Body without a body.

This is a body, a body!
Body of wonder,
body of hope.
Body of oceans,
body of harbors.

This is a body enfleshed,
like yours. This is a body
broken, like mine. See how
we stutter through rubble,
wounded, till we fall.

This is a body of words,
a body of history,
a body of knowledge.
This is a body of fact
and a body of lies.

Here are the bodies
sprawled in the street
like puppets. The bodies
dangling in frantic peril
from ravaged roofs.

Here are the bodies
seized. The bodies fleeing.
The bodies that stay alive
with eyes that burn, limbs torn off.
The bodies in which we die.

This is a vessel of flesh,
a shipwrecked hull.
Here is the gasping breath,
the vanishing shore.
Here are the ones who drowned.

Originally published in ***Vox Populi****, Oct. 23, 2023*

Ya 'Amar

My friend sends me photos of children
lost to bombs, their still-living faces
shining like moons –*ya 'amar!*– in hopes
I will write poems to keep them alive.
They are not lost, of course, but murdered,
torn to bits. Sometimes, we hide in language
to make it through – though the children
had nowhere to hide and didn't survive.
Searching for words to stem the grief,
I scroll through images, wincing at
fresh young faces, the smiling eyes –
people smiled in Gaza, I swear, despite
everything. The pictures are easier to take
than my news feed's cruel contortions:
hands protruding from rubble, forearms
and legs inscribed with names so that
victims can be identified when beheaded by
the rain of bombs. The children laughing
into the camera, hugging siblings or parents,
clutching a toy or ball or schoolbag, demand
we refuse their destruction. Their shining eyes
gaze out, trusting those beyond the lens
to keep them safe, whole, alive. They do not
know, yet, how this will end: faces smeared
with blood, hands clutching soot, bodies
cradled in a ragged heap by grievers
who rock in anguished keening. At one
bombing site, a girl lifted alive from
the moonscape of devastation cries out
to her rescuer, "Ammo, are you taking me
to the cemetery?" He exclaims tenderly,
"Cemetery, what cemetery! Look at you,
child, you are alive and beautiful like the moon!"

But beyond them, the lunar arc etched into
Gaza's black and broken sky is barely visible:
ya 'amar, the sky is so dark, ya 'amar,
the light has left us, where is the moon?

Originally published in **Literatura Scripta,** *27, 61, June 2024.*

-

Shroud of Light

If I must die, you must live to tell my story
Refaat Alareer

By the time they killed Refaat, there was nothing new
about the rows of bodies rolled up in stark white shrouds,
surprisingly unbesmirched by dust or blood, tied

at both ends in neat bundles, sometimes in the middle
too, so the sheet wouldn't slip, carried gently through
streets on the way to mass graves, those pits dug

in whatever ground could be reached without the living
being picked off by snipers, the unstained white
of winding cloths belying the odor of carnage

permeating every crevice, miasma of death hanging
like an ashen pall in the sky, clogging the lungs of those
who still try to breathe. A newscaster said *children*

are meant to play in the dirt, but in Gaza, it's their shroud.
Even that is beyond many. One Gazan wrote, *if I die,*
please make sure my children's bodies are covered –

not left open to wild dogs, the relentless, howling
sky. Lost beneath rubble, Refaat was denied
a poet's burial left only stone dust and concrete

for his shroud. But the words that survive his death
wrap his living spirit in a gauze of light.
"There's a Palestine that dwells inside all of us,"

he wrote. Take his words, inscribe them on a kite,
brilliant white, to fly high over the terrible world,
so that his death is a tale that brings hope,

so that he lives, so that we live, so that Gaza
becomes a place not of shrouds but of freedom,
kites rippling in sunshine, lit by the blaze of life.

*Originally published in **Rattle, Poets Respond**, December 2023.*

What We Carry

There is no bearing this weight
but she carries it anyway: little sister
slung like a rucksack across her shoulder,
broken leg dangling, her own eyes limned
with dark shadows, blond hair falling
across her face like a curtain,
gap-toothed attempt at a smile.

As she speaks, she shifts her bundle
of sister – not a burden, not heavy.
She has already trudged kilometers,
shouldering this load beyond her years.
Both girls are small and frail. Too young
for this world, they have only each other:
barefoot childbearing her sister down the road.

Where are they going? How will they live?
The younger child needs a doctor. Her sister
needs.... a different universe, a safety net,
a living parent, bread, a jug of water.
But there is no clean water in Gaza,
their parents are dead, their home demolished,
and nothing grows in the rubble.

From afar, we carry this knowledge,
a stone we cannot put down.
We bear despair and grief and rage,
the guilt of helplessness,
the pulse of hope already broken.
We bear the urgency of witness,
the fragility of what is human.

Who can help these children stay alive?
Who can stop the dark from seizing them?
The older girl hoists her sister, this burden
that is not a burden, hunches herself into
the weight of love, and walks.

MARWAN MAKHOUL
Hello Beit Hanoun

Hello!
Beit Hanoun?
I heard on the news
that an artisan baker has come
to distribute bread
on the back of fresh artillery.
I also heard
that one of his loaves feeds
at least twenty children
and is so warm it burns, and solid
like a randomly targeted shell.
They said:
Children woke up early that day
not to go to school
but to the local youth club
opposite the town's playground
that in summer is big enough for two massacres
and a certain hope, the hope to live.
I also heard
that when they were on their way
they neglected their wounds
and poured blood on corners
until blood became the colour of the streets
and feelings.
When I saw what I saw on the screen
I thought I was dreaming
or the TV was dreaming the impossible made real.
I never imagined Beit Hanoun,
that you'd mean anything to me,
what with all the fun I'm having
like being busy with friends discussing
whether wine in the bottle
ferments or not.

I never knew you'd mean anything to me,
even something small
something small, Beit Hanoun.
Hello...?
Hello...?
Beit Hanoun?
Can you hear me?
I think the phone's not working
or perhaps has gone to sleep,
it is very late, after all.
Never mind, let it go.
I've nothing better to do
than catch up with my brothers shading themselves
by the axed trunk of Arab solidarity.
Goodbye, Beit Hanoun.
Goodbye.

Translated by Raphael Cohen

New Gaza

No time left
so don't linger in your mother's womb
my little boy hurry arrive
not because I long for you
but because war is raging
I fear you will not see
your country as I'd wish for you.
...
Your country is not soil
nor sea that foresaw our fate and died:
it is your people.
Come get to know it
before the bombs mutilate
and I am forced to gather the remains
for you to know that those gone were beautiful
and innocent.
That they had children just like you
they let escape
from the freezers for the dead
at every raid to skip as orphans
on a lifeline.
...
If you're late, you may not
believe me and believe it is a land
without a people
and that we were not really here at all.
Twice exiled, then we revolted
against our luck
for seventy-five years
once luck turned all bad
and hope turned grey.
...

The burden's too heavy
too much for you to bear
I know, forgive me for like a gazelle
giving birth, I am afraid
of hyenas lying in wait to pounce behind
the pit. Come quick then run
as far as you can
so I'm not ravaged by regret.
...

Last night, despair exhausted me
I said, keep quiet.
What's it to do with him?
My little one, child of the breeze,
what's the Storm to do with him?
But today, I am compelled to come back
bearing breaking news:
They bombed the Baptist Hospital in Gaza
among the 500 victims was a child
who calls to his brother, half his head blown off
eyes open: "My brother!
Can you see me?"
He does not see him
just like the frantic world
that condemned for two hours then slept
to forget him
and forget his brother
does not see him.
...

What to tell you now?
Disaster and catastrophe are sisters
both ravenous and raging, they attack me
until my lips tremble, and from them drop
all possible synonyms for
corpse.
In time of war don't count on any poet
he's as slow as a tortoise
making a futile effort to race a massacre
that runs like a hare.
The tortoise creeps
and the hare leaps from crime to crime
as far as the Orthodox Church, now bombed
in the sight of God, who's just come from
a mosque razed to dust they targeted
in the sanctuary of the saviour. Where is the saviour
when our Father who art in heaven actually is the
airplane, one alone and with no partner
save the one on board who came to bomb us
but the target hit is our submission.
My child, on the cross now
there's enough room for all the prophets.
God knows all
but you and innocent foetuses like you
are yet to know.

Translated by Raphael Cohen

The Exodus from Ireland

I arrived in Ireland, and my coat cried out:
You've gone abroad, my friend, but left me at home!
Perhaps it was an omen,
for missiles were embracing over my family
in Galilee when I weakened and accepted Annemarie's invitation.
I came to read my poems, here, to ones far away,
poems that at first hearing made the local translator
betray them and sob.
Perhaps they reminded him of his grandfather
who eluded oppression before me
a century ago until he gained liberation
and independence.

I grew up very sensitive to the cold
my mother is the one to blame
rushing over to wrap me up whenever
she heard the slightest rumble of thunder.
On the three-day trip, whenever
they offered me a break between readings,
I would flee to the shops of Dublin,
where there's no shortage of
luxury brands, whose prices made me dizzy
so I hurried back to the next reading
to get my circulation going and calm down.
That, my family in Galilee, is how I spent my
trip, feeling the warmth of those around me
– I mean those demonstrating to stop the war –
their gasps blanketing me as if they were cattle
over the manger where I was an envoy sent by a Jesus
believing like me in the poem.

Ireland, you were closer to me than myself.
I forgot the cold that returned with my return,
the day I bought a coat in Frankfurt airport, ice-cold
like Germany's stance on a holocaust raising groans of pain
from those displaced from north of Gaza to south of Gaza

to a camp being immolated right now
on another final frontier in Rafah.
Thank you, Ireland
and damn those who apologize for the distant past
while they turn a blind eye to my present, whose future
is a shame on those like them, but I am not going away
and so the shame will never go away.

Translated by: Raphael Cohen

Portrait of the Family of Gaza

The bitter ruins of Gaza
sprouted the arm of a child.
It waved at God two days ago
but the heavens were overcast
as their symbolic resonance had been rented to jets
to render that hand,
pregnant with the phoenix
of the ashes, and so-called hope,
invisible.
Last night, I convinced myself to sleep
and not watch television.
I saw beyond the imagination of one with wounded dreams:
The dogs in Rafah
were tasting pain.
Our wounded childhood
was begging a dog:
"Kill me,"
so feelings might have a reprieve from the jackboot.
Death, who sent you?
Who swept away the clouds of deepest winter, so their
vultures could be seen swooping down to the brink of life?
Death,
seek not the children,
depart.
They've gone on their own to the chilled compartments of the morgue.
All their loved ones are there, staying up late.
On the top level, their mother, Hasna,
dies hurriedly
to stake a place in the graveyard for her little ones.
Death, who recommended me?
Death ...
How long have you been looking out for your children at school?
You know they're not there.
Didn't your amateur wildness tell you it's a holy day?
Let me ask you ...

Where are the prophets of old
to deliver the victims from the guileless bullet?
The house next door has no room for salvation ...
By the God who made grief a joke
before my eyes,
and who made my assailant laugh at me,
I can see the unseeable.
Bewail the slaughtered my truce-seeking heart and take note
of the calibre of the gun and the world's silence.
Forget atonement,
time and again, you have slaughtered me tolerantly
and howled at nothing.
The Gospels are meaningless, not wiping away the tears of the wound
on the day the butcher endlessly flays my skin.* So I continue
in agony, the mystique having fallen away.
Merciful one, tell me
are you ignorant of the modern warmonger?
Do you equate the sword of tribesmen to the bomb?
By God, speak!
Has he who loves you won?
By God,
answer!

Translated by Raphael Cohen

---

* See Qur'an 4:56, "Surely those who disbelieve in Our signs – We shall certainly roast them at a Fire; as often as their skins are wholly burned, we shall give them in exchange other skins, that they may taste the chastisement. Surely God is All-mighty, All-wise."

An Arab at Ben Gurion Airport

I'm an Arab!
I shouted, at the doorway to departures,
short-cutting the woman soldier's path to me.
I went up to her and said: Interrogate me! But
quickly, if you don't mind. I don't want to miss
take-off time.

She said: Where are you from?
Descended from Ghassassanian kings of Golan is my heroism, I said.
My neighbour was Rehab, the harlot of Jericho
who gave Joshua the wink on his way to the West Bank
the day he occupied the land that occupied history after him
from the very first page.
My answers are as stony as Hebron granite:
I was born in the time of the Moabites who came down before you
to this submissive ancient land.
My father a Canaanite
my mother a Phoenician, from South Lebanon of old.
My mother, her mother died two months ago
and she was unable to see her mother off two months ago.
I wept in her arms so that on-looking from Buqaya might console
the worst blow of tragedy and fate:
Lebanon, you see impossible sister,
and my mother's mother alone
to the north!

She asked me: Who packed your bag for you?

I said: Osama Ibn Laden! But hold on,
take it easy. It's no more than a joke in poor taste,
a quip that the realists here, like me use professionally
for the struggle.
Sixty years I've fought with words about peace.
I don't attack the settlement
and I don't have a tank like you do
ridden by a soldier to tickle Gaza.

Dropping a bomb from an Apache isn't on my CV
not because I lack qualifications,
no, but because I see on the horizon a ripple echoing
enough to the out-of-place revolt of the non-violent
and to good behaviour.

Did anyone give you something on the way here? she asked.

I said: An exile from Nayrab refugee camp
gave me memories
and the key to a house from the fabled past.
The rust on the key made me edgy, but I'm
like stainless steel, I compose self with self should I grow nostalgic,
for the groans of refugees
spread wings of longing across borders.
No guard can stop it, nor thousands
and not you for sure.

She said: Do you have any sharp implements in your possession?

I said: My passion
my skin, my olive complexion
my being born here in innocence, but for fate.
Pess-optimistic I was in the seventies
but I'm optimistic about the roars of disobedience
right now being raised to you in Gilboa gaol.
I'm straight out of the
tragic novels of history, the end of the story
a funeral for the past and a wedding
in the not-far-off hall of hope.
A raisin from the Jordan Valley raised me
and taught me to speak.
I have a child whose due date I postponed, so he'll arrive
to a morning not made of straw like today, daughter of Ukraine.
The muezzin's chanting moves me, even though I'm an atheist.
I shout to mute the mournful wailing of the flutes,
to turn pistols into the undying strains of violins.

The soldier took me to search my things
ordering me to open my bag.
I do what she wants!
And from the depths of the bag ooze my heart and my song,
the meaning of it all slips out eloquently and crudely,
    within it all that is me.

She asked me: And what's this?

I said: The sura of the Night Journey ascending the ladder of my veins,
the Tafsir of Jalalayn,
the poetry of Abu Tayyeb al-Mutannabi and my sister Maram,
as a photograph and real at the same time,
a silk shawl to enwrap and protect me from the chill exile of relatives,
tobacco from a kiosk in Arraba that made my head spin until
    doubts got stoned.
Inside me, a fierce loyalty, the wild thyme of my country,
the fieriness of pomegranate blossoms, Galilean and sparkling.
Inside me agate, camphor-wood, incense, and my being alive,
the pearl that is Haifa: scintillating, everlasting, illuminating,
preposterous, relaxing in the pocket of our return for one reason
only: we worshipped our good intentions and bound
the *nakba* to a slip in the past and in me!

The soldier hands me over to a policeman
who pats me down and shouts in surprise:
What's this!?

The manhood of my nation, I say
and my progeny, the fold of my family and two dove's eggs
to hatch, male and female, from me and for me.
He searches me
for anything that could pose a threat
but this stranger is blind
forgetting the more destructive and important bombs within:
my spirit, my defiance, the swoop of the hawk in my breath and my body

my birthmark and my valour. That is me
whole and complete in a way this fool
will never see.

Now, after two hours of psychological grappling
I lick my wounds for a sufficient five minutes
then embark on the plane that has taken off. Not to leave
and not to return
but to see the soldier below me
the policeman in the national anthem of my shoes below me
and below me a big lie of tin-can history
like Ben Gurion become as always, as always, as always
below me.

Translated by Raphael Cohen

LEILA MARSHY
Exit Visa

There are ways of thinking
I have discovered recently
that have nothing to do with
me, and by me, I really mean
you, who has colonized
my thoughts with little flags
one for every tract of land you rip in half
red for the massacres you aspire to
whipping in the wind with indignation
your favourite feeling, by the way
in Dig Nation
you, number one citizen
dictator, dissident and destroyer rolled into one.
The chosen one.

So, what I am thinking is this:
The land rolls like a body under my touch
a little pressure, and it pushes back
like sponge or warm skin or moss.
I am going to take off my clothes and lie in it
and not worry for a second
about the enemy.
This, I suddenly realize, is escape.

Kinship

I finally know why
I feel a kinship with the Jews:
They have made me one of them.
My Palestinian family live
where they are not wanted,
my father was exiled for no reason
other than all of a sudden what was his
was not.
Just like the Jews
we wear our ethnicity on a piece of cloth
and an entire country has decided
we need to be rounded up
and herded out.
Just like the Jews
the walls built to crush us
can barely contain us.
And now, just like the Jews,
we are being blamed and vilified
and hounded and hunted
and exterminated.
For centuries, the Jews were alone in the world;
lucky for them, they have made us in their image.

Originally published in the **Canadian Dimension**, *January 14, 2024.*

Where Is My Country?

Where is my goddamn country
whose floods disarm roads and
neighbours track the shame
of torn bras and underwear in the rain
don't you look, don't you turn away
don't you leave this is my country
let me see your travel papers
thwak! my stamp my face, my words
my language impossible to leave without it
promises to detain me
I'm not going anywhere today.

Where is my country?
The one I wrote about but in the wrong
accent saying things I never meant
as the wheels sucked up the clay from the riverbed
and sprayed it onto our faces
hardening into masks that hurt when we smiled
not that we tried, it wasn't that kind of wild
it was the time you held out your hands
at the border crossing and the agent said
I know another name we can call you and that was that
you fled like the coward you are, my history
is full of people like you.

Where is my country?
A cliff leaning against the ocean where you hold my arms
behind my back and spread my legs
for inspection with the tip of your soft boot
you ask where was I born
who were my parents, why did I leave
who sent me in, whom do I believe
until it's too much even for you and
my laughter cuts your serious face
to pieces.

Where is my country?
Too many allegiances what a luxury to have
just one language, one religion, one mountain
one valley, one lover, you know, *that* country
the one we saw in a movie
where he smiled like a compass
and she said look at me like you mean it
look at me like you know me
like your dreams aren't full of weaponry
like the length of your arms aren't a boundary
and he did, and when no one
was watching, she handed
him her passport
and crossed.

*Originally published in **Font Magazine**, April 2022*

AHMED MIQDAD
O Sea

I'm a displaced Palestinian
who resides on your wide beach
fleeing from human brutality.

O sea,
I beg you, please raise your voice
and make your waves so rough
to cover this genocide
and lessen the sounds of massive bombs.

O sea,
humanity abandoned us
homeless inside a tent
your sand is our warm cuddle.

Picturesque

I am

sitting on the beach
listening to the music of waves and seashells
alleviating the warcrafts' sounds

gazing at the green rocks in the clear water
feeling the immaculate heart of the sea
ruminating the purity of its thoughts
to run away from falsified truth
that humanity has a heart

enjoying the sunsets
the silver clouds that draw the view
eliminating the images of killed children

counting the stars all night
waiting the new tranquil dawn
hoping humanity wakes up again.

Don't Count

Don't count me as a number
I'm a soul flying in my kindergarten
playing with my toys

Don't count me as a number
I'm a beautiful rose
colouring my parents' lives

Don't count me as a number
I'm a beating heart
with love and peace

Don't count me as a number
I'm a fighting father
protecting my children with my bare body

Don't count me as a number
I'm a mourning mother
shedding tears over the shrines of the beloved lost

Don't count me as a number
I'm a martyr with family and friends
feeling my absence among them

Don't count me as a number
the notorious army demolishes my home
I am exhausted from your silence.

If I Were

If I were your daughter
Would you like to see my tears on my cheeks?!
If I were your wife
Would you like to hear me mourn?!
If I were your son
Would you like to watch my amputated limbs?!
If I were your olive tree
Would you like to torch me?!
If I were your brother
Would you like to capture me behind bars?!
If I were your sister
Would you like to violate my honor?!
If I were your mother
Would you like to make me a widow?!
If I were your father
Would you like to humiliate me?!
If I were your neighbor
Would you like to kill me?!
If I were the dream
Why would you like to be the nightmare?!
If I were the hope
Why would you like to be the despair?!
If I were the love
Why would you like to be the despised?!
If I were life
Why would you like to wish me death?!

Where Am I from?

I am

from the land of prophets
where they ascended to heavens

I'm from the land of olive trees and citrus
where guests are generously hosted

I'm from the farm of love
that grows passion and affection

I'm from the land of minarets
where the bell and Azhan are brothers

I'm from the land of gathering and resurrection
where justice will prevail

I'm from Al-Aqsa, Jerusalem, Hebron, Haifa, Jaffa and Gaza
with the glamorous sky and the azure sea

I'm from the land of good people
where the clouds rain goodness and honesty

I'm from the color of sun and the Dome of Rock
where the tyranny collapses

I'm from the land of my grandparents' history and tales
where the memory is still sharp and awake

I'm from the land of martyrs
all in a deadly procession

I'm from the land of irony where the colonizers fall
I'm from Palestine!

MARIA MIRAGLIA
Gaza

My heart bleeds from the pain
that would explode
like fireworks
to light up the skies
of towns and countries
 to show they have no boundaries

Make it visible to the blinded
by cruelty and greed
that the clouds and stars
don't wave flags
all men living under the same sky

And then cry out
my joy for life
but all my anger, too
and shout against the powerful
to awaken their conscience

If only I could
stretch out my hands
to caress the children in Gaza
dry their mothers' tears
share the sorrows of men
outraged in their souls and bodies
and sing with them hymns of peace.

WALID NABHAN
Gaza's Golgotha

Gaza is crucified on the cross of Golgotha
abandoned naked in the hurling wind
every time she attempts to cover her thighs
she finds only her children's bodies
from which she weaves blankets

In the morning of Gaza,
and the morning has been since the morning,
he paints history with nails made of metal
so, in the calendar of humanity
he marks a new Feast
that celebrates the victory over the refugees.
Blessed are they who grabs what is theirs from their blood
blessed are they who fill their pockets from their thirst
blessed is every spear that pierced their babies
Eli, my God, Elohim
why have you abandoned the refugees?

Gaza's evening
on the hill of the bloody Golgotha
her pants pulled down
her breasts slashed
dripping salt and sulphur
and the fingers of silence
rummaging her private parts.

How many times do I have to suffocate from the smoke
of the cannons of democracy?
Why do I have to bear the swords of silence?

Translated by John P. Portelli

MIRELA NECULA
We Have the Right, the Right to...

I deeply believe
that it fits in the tiny suitcase of thin memories
a dignified and immaculate time of love
like the incredibly long drumlins
with only dreams, sun and long sky,

And I shout with the voice of heaven that wants us
we have the right, the right to...
that the foundation of life and love reins
silent as the sunrise in the streams
and the luggage is full, like dirt with slops
of my happiness, of wandering stream
either is heaven, either is rod and sun, and rain.

And the time will come when will come out
that we have the right, the right to...
that certain Dacian flowers,
in love, wants to get dressed
with dark circles to make peace
and with the flashed rain of mulled kisses
I choose the mystery of Christianized feathers.

My happiness, the fire chariot of little life
we have the right, the right to the last chance of good
going up one step, up two essences
it intersects, like a heaven long ago, a new world
sign that I left at the last hand
and that the long alpenhorn looks good with a brake

Tuck Me in

Come home, autumn is coming, wind is coming
All that was left behind has faded away, it is broken
In the background, the calm and restlessness kisses cowardly
And the blind tear speaks...

Autumn is coming, it's coming crooked, hasty
Smiling through the maze of every poppy
The love delirium blooms alone, lightheaded
And without you I return, silent, sob, what should I do?

"You won't be able to give me a hand
I'm going to fall and you won't be able to"
Watery autumn to keep it straight, to the dead
"I'm going to fall, and you won't be able to."

Late if you arrive, tuck me in
With as much peace as long as your love boils
With her arms and rivers beneath the stature of the evening
It seeks my warm breathing and hold me to the bosom of resurrection

MANSOUR NOORBAKHSH
My Journey
For the Children of Gaza

It was somewhere in the middle of my way,
where I sat down.
I didn't stop.
But I was not able to move.

Perhaps in the spiral of a tall staircase.
That rises as far as the steps exist.
where my father had stopped as a child.

Or maybe in the middle of a deep well,
where the steps fall to the absolute darkness.
where my mother had fallen as a child.

I sat down. I didn't stop.
I fenced my face with my hands
to protect my eyes
from the slaps of shadows that were rising
from my past to mock my future.

JOSEPH C. OGBONNA
The Israel-Gaza War

On October the 7th the precarious peace
of the disputed ancient lands began to cease.
The enraged avengers brought the Al-Aqsa flood
that deluged the Re'im music festival with blood.

Then, very swiftly came the lopsided response
that decimated women and children at once.
The Zionists' war machine sweeps the Gazan land,
rendering its closely compacted earth to flatland.

The mosques, churches, schools and hospitals are all gone.
Scores wail uncontrollably aloud as they mourn.
Having no point of refuge, refugees take flight
as they seek for bomb shelters with no hopes in sight.

Hamas belligerents their explosive arrows throw
at overwhelmed defenses of an age-old foe.
Zionists with torrential explosives respond
with offensive operations within and beyond.

Oh, that the Gaza strip might tranquility know!
Oh, that the blood in the West bank would cease to flow!
Oh, that Israel would flourish and as a nation grow!
Oh, that the warring factions would the seed of peace sow!
Oh, that the two warring parties would merry and dance!
Oh, that the two-state solution was given a chance!

Mother Gaza

A percentage of me has to hell been consigned
by the ever-raging Zionists' war machine.
To each livid soldier, a mandate is assigned
to uproot terror where multitudes are confined.
Torrents of explosives have swept our landscapes clean.
Churches, mosques, schools have all to mighty vengeance bowed.
Stricken mothers wail uncontrollably aloud.
Itinerancy pervades my horror-stricken crowd,
whilst my kids toy with explosives, carnage and ruin.
Survivors will take shelter from snipers shooting
death balls and lead from peevish and portable guns.
Horror unprecedented the people outruns.
I have metamorphosed to nothing but a morgue.
Lice and bugs have infested hoodies lined with borg.
Diseased and maimed limbs have no remedies in sight.
Let not the world be unmoved by my sorry plight.
Why must I this price pay for a thousand or more killed?
My morgues are beyond their capacity filled.
The deaths of innocents are nothing but unjust.
My once-populated streets have been turned to dust.

MUHAMMED HÜSEYIN ÖZER
Once upon a Time

To be honest, I have never heard a tale that begins with once upon a time.
My whole story ended with my mother's scream.
Since the moment I existed, I have been pushed into the journey of extinction.

But how would you even know?
While I was running from cluster bombs,
I breathed in the apple-scented phosphorus.

The beginning and the end of my story are the same.
My fate has a single face –
The time between my existence and my disappearance,
The life measured out for me, is death itself.
I have never heard a tale that begins with once upon a time.

I spent countless days hidden under a blanket,
Hiding behind the same side of the fabric day after day.
I watched the light shatter into pieces at night,
Heard the footsteps of those seeking refuge in the flying glow.
I held back the demons that emerged from those very feet.

While the light revealed its terrifying face,
I knotted the seconds in my throat.
I never wasted my time sobbing.
Not against death, no…
It was the light I resisted.
I have never heard a tale that begins with once upon a time.

I built castles out of stone, watched clouds of dust rise.
To escape drowning, I hid in a fortress of stone.
Centuries-old battles crushed beneath the tracks,
Honor is lost, conscience erased – my home left in ruins.
While men with long shadows covered my sky,
My brother, my mother – there is no one left in this pit.

I cannot push my hatred uphill with a toy car in my hand.
I am the orphan of my land, a hero who died bravely.
I have never heard a tale that begins with once upon a time.

Translated by Kadir Tepe

GIANNA PATRIARCA
Controllers

the front-row seats are never reserved
for those who build them
                       or repair them
or wash them or set them up   neatly
side by side like soldiers for inspection
before the war

that North American dream
was never   free
it came with an enormous price tag
and a lifetime mortgage
with an option to purchase   souls

those who have a need to control
and an appetite for power
cannot bear the word   love
it is much too radical
                it is uncontrollable
it has no fear
so they choose the word   hate
it is so much easier to feed hate
to the masses
it is full of fear   and terror

JOHN P. PORTELLI
You Swallow Your Anger

Today, like yesterday and always
you swallow the anger accumulated
over years of exile in your homeland,
you lose sense of time
constantly surrounded by the dead,
and the smell reminds me of the smoke of Auschwitz.

Bodies are bodies.
After death, differences do not matter –
sobbing and pity are of no worth.

Suddenly, as always, the ground shook
the tent flapping frantically with every wind,
searching for a spot without graves –
but to no avail.
Your destiny is too harsh.
Even the ground has gotten used to the stains of children
slaughtered on the boiling sand.

With a lump in your throat,
you gather the lonely shoe of your daughter,
not to place it in the museum
but so her siblings may remember her
if they are lucky enough
to live another hour.

Dreaming of Tomorrow

You sent me a photo of the pitch darkness
under your tent, trying to clutch to yesterday's dreams

the rain pouring incessantly
the dreams freezing

and now the floor in the tent overflowing
may be the dreams will turn into ice

the smoke of the lonely fire disappeared
it's insufferable to dream of tomorrow

After the Genocide

Your kindness is endless
even the snow melts on your frigid grave
and the withered leaves slide into nothingness

you wrote to me
we survived the genocide –
maybe, after all, hope is
conceivable

in silent meditation
I released the shawl of my life.

Pretense

I pretend to be strong to make them feel safe and secure
A friend from Gaza

between you and me a huge abyss
an occasional note that breaks the heart

putting on a false front is tough
a mountain ready to collapse

your deep sorrow contained and calm
your hope radiates zeal

the silence between one land and another
terrifies the ghosts buried in the sand

the coffee pot in the tent is empty
today, only the shadows dare to stroll on the beach

Hope?

The Pope is praying for the year of hope
and you are finding refuge under a frigid tent
huddling your dear children for warmth
asking when will this life of theirs change –
a life daily blooded by the death of their friends
with whom once they played in the garden
full of lemon and orange blossoms.
How can I console you when you tell me
that you are living only the moment, if you survive,
always scavenging for some flour and water?

NILOY RAFIQ
The Bellicose

A march of deaths!

Tender roses fall in the door of fate,
Red maps are drawn by the Krishnachura flowers.

The barbarism of the early ages resurrected
human beings just spectators in the playground.

While the protests of dreamers resound
Looters killing in cold blood, draw dreams in a cup of wine with an exultation.

The window of the empire simpers!

Translated by Jyotirmoy Nandy

SHIRANI RAJAPAKSE
On the Beach

And when the smoke cleared
they saw the child lying on the sand like a
piece of paper crumpled and thrown
into the trash. Salt winds ruffled his hair,
the waters beyond beckoned.
"Come into me,
    come,
        come into me"
the waves whispered running
in and out, waiting
for him to get up and run.
Run like he was doing before he fell.
Run like he wanted to race into her cool embrace.
Run like it was the better place to be.
But his feet
had stopped moving
his eyes stopped seeing.
He no longer heard the voices of the sea,
sounds of gulls in the air.
The roar of guns silenced inside his head.
Forever.
And as they ran towards him, their
child, they saw the earth stick out her tongue
and begin to sip him in.
Slowly, slowly she drank him in drop by
little drop of red quenching the earth,
and around him lay the others stopped in play
feeding the earth, staring up, up.
And as the cry rose from their throats and they beat
their breasts in vain falling to the ground
to ask what
mad God would do such
to his sons, the skies started to howl anew
as madness rained down once again.

Originally published in **Dove Tales, Writing for Peace,** *2017, USA.*

Somewhere in Gaza

I don't remember my room anymore.
The one I grew up in, played games.
We fought, my sister and I
wanting the spot in front of the window,
sitting on the ledge to watch
the world go by,
unwilling to give up
our cherished place to the other, even
for a moment.
Birds trilled outside, and we tried to
mimic their song, but they only laughed
at our vain attempt.
It took years for the men
to build the walls,
paint them,
clean the floors, make it ready to live.
Then came the bombs...
The walls shuddered in fear as the roof
opened its mouth wide and screamed
in shock.
My room, I shared with my sister.
My room, I played with my cousins.
My room, our father
built that day in the beautiful place close
to the olive trees that bent
their branches for us to play.
Rubble all around, pieces of pink wall
turned ugly and dark
crane necks to stare sadly
at the sky
through the roof's gaping mouth,
wondering what other gifts
it will hurl down in wrath.
Leaning against a piece of my room,
I sing out to the birds, but they have
flown away

and will not return
to recount stories of distant
places only they can visit.
No restrictions, no imprisonment.
They can move
beyond the walls of hate
while I remain
trapped.
But now that, too, is a mirage
crumbling in front of my eyes.

Originally published in **The Way It Is** *(2024), Sri Lanka.*

Hope

Sometimes, the sun smiles through holes in the roof,
that piece of plastic shielding us
blowing messages of sadness from other
places, scattering our words to winds.
If I had a bottle, I'd store my memories inside
and fling it far into the ocean, but they are all
shattered like my dreams every night.
Sometimes.
Sometimes I wonder what it's like to walk
outside to the silence
not see men with guns growing out of their arms,
taste freedom on the air, and not breathe in
the foul stench of gun powder or
the stink of death calling, calling.
It's just a dream that disappears
when I awaken to the sound of war howling outside
my window.
Sometimes, I wish I was somewhere else
and I didn't have to
grow up so soon.
Sometimes hope is all that's left, but that's begun to
disappear like the piece of photograph of my
grandmother that's
turning the color of old paper,
dirty brown and fading.

*Originally published in **The Way It Is** (2024), Sri Lanka.*

GIOVANNA RICCIO
The Mother of All Bombs

The Mother of all Bombs cozy in a paternal bearhug. Adoring warmonger prez himself adored by his double. The Mother's double spirited by the duo crashes in a pas a deux with its doubles. The Mother restless, eyeing Palestinian boys and girls. Their hands that reached for Motherlove...
Earsplittingthunderousroar. Megabomb fire flash hellish smoke blooms a Newsflash. No evidence of war crimes, declares the Press Secretary. Babes crushed. Body piles on screens at the military museum. War's worn-out shoes waiting, tiny dismembered feet of Gazan children land in piles of shoes at the Auschwitz Museum. Mothers' bones clamouring beneath rumbling homes. Bloodlines collapsing in rubbled bones. Mothers ululating, their mouths bleeding names. Crushed names, crimson lips, wails of newborns flail for dead mothers. The Mother of All Bombs crimsons their cries. The afterimage bloodying screens. Screens we wipe clean each day. No evidence.

My House

The struggle against power is the struggle against forgetting
Milan Kundera

Downing storms lift night
a new morning breaks through rubble – rescues
me from dreams deafened by F-16 fighter jets,
deadened by MK-84 mega-bombs

from twilight's empire
of twisted rebar, pulverized stone, the living stench
of burnt-to-the-bone toddlers, cradled
in the arms of fragmented mothers
Where to rest slaughtered love
in this calendar weeping butchered tomorrows?

Clearing a new day of oxygen-starved newborns
the addled street sweeper recites multiplication tables,
and the intrepid doctor's tear-soaked words ascend
a hanging staircase rising to open sky
above one more mangled school....

No darkly brewed coffee muffles dawn's red flags
flapping in his plea, *we are dying now, hear me....*

And while the street sweeper reimagines
torched oleanders, tenderly gathers
the death count mounting outside besieged Al Shifa Hospital
nails it to the doors of the Knesset and White House,
exponential body bags press against my door –
it's my bell, the disremembered murdered ring.

And all the while, a naked girl races through my hallways.
Skin seared by Napalm's sooty bloom, she flees
into the TV's all-consuming lens – on her heels,
a train of scalded children,
moms cradling limp babes in their arms.

and like recurrent echoes of a barbed heartbeat,
a skeletal girl clad in Auschwitz stripes
and her knobby-kneed twin riffle my kitchen,

hands stuffed with bread, oranges and history,
they sit cross-legged before the blazing fireplace,

in the flames, their grieved mother flickers
her glittering blue eyes and powerful arms
shield a Palestinian newborn

sister and brother call, call again, frantic
to guide her home

                    as mother
                    and child   float off
                    chimney smoke scarring the blue.

OMAR SABBAGH
The Unimaginable

We all do it: scrolling down the hand-held screen,
letting passages of words without sounding breaths
pass-over us like a see-through shroud.
And as we clock with some small, shy part of our intelligence,
the horrors committed this side of death or not –

cramming our mouths with our pettiness, muzzling the loud
shrieks we might've shrieked had we not been there
to see such things come to pass, over and over –

we return once more to the impossible: that we cannot
turn back the acid of the snaking clock, shadowy, colorless;
that we cannot rewind time's stone-hard beeline or light
a tunnel beneath the ground for the succouring
of those who stay to live above it, suffering what they are;
that we cannot un-pierce the rabid sting
the damned prolong, busy othering the same darned blood
into their wished-for color – the utter black that is the might
and folly of their hollowed conquest; that we cannot...

And perhaps we might pity the worldly victor more
as we watch him seam the mainland story, connect the dots
in what will always be a travesty of the imagination
and of all the futures that even one mind alone possessed
before barrenness made the land and genocide
screamed the words for this one-manned liturgy of murder.

Peace

What is it, and what does it look like?
Is it a pear, or is it an apple? Plum? Peach?
What is its color when it's fully awake,
when it's fully there? Is it a kind of a mess, or is it neat?
Is it true to itself, always, from mind to foot,
and when it swims with people inside of it, is it
more like a lake or river, or is it a bursting cloud?
Or is it like a sea made to make of all things harsh and loud,
softer, smoother fare? I am just a man
searching the bowers, he knows to understand
what home is like, that cushioned space that's made
for hope and one's endless return, again and again, a place
where one might lay one's head down in rest at the last
and find sleep like half a glass of water become a fuller, unfinished one.

Christmas, 2023

There are no more saints inside the morning air
and no more wizened scholars either.
Shame walks the wind between us, and its gusts
speak in tongues of abandonment, of lovelessness.
God goes, forced to die another day, the daylight
falls, shedding its leaves of golden brightness
like a snake its aged skin. We are being untaught
again, our minds blanketed, razed – as the innocent
fall beneath the weight, like final strangers, of eerie gifts.
This is no season of hope, of green, of white, of sap-like uplift,
the dying, even more than the massive dead, sent
from life, still living, and the figurations of sense
build from a zero-brick, arks thin as wafts of saddened mint
in a world without flowers, the only growth we have, descent.

Lost Sundays

I do not pray or keep the keep
that others may. The only thing I see
to be hallowed are high and jagged walls.
In this, I am like most of the world
I know. So that Sunday means very little
to me, and no martyr drives the way
forward, splitting wide-lipped seas or walking
upon them. And the emanating rays
of the morning sun and the chill breeze,
mean nothing special, apart from nothing.
To the west of me, a nation burns,
hoodwinked and suffering and seized
by the shame of never having had its turn
even to fail, desperately, at being a nation.

PAUL SALVATORI
heartless state

smear you for
telling the truth

they would end your life, too

mention "genocide" and they
lash out

intolerant of what's real

amid the atrocities
broadcast to the world
where the perpetrator is clear

they still insist
they are the victim

insulting the dead
the blood of every martyr
soaking gaza ground

wrath

the little boy is crying
for his mother
but she is dead
shrapnel from the bomb
intended for them both
pierced her everywhere
while she covered him with
her body
trying to save him
from a rotten wrath that
she – whose home was open to anyone – could never understand

northern migration

they are walking home now. and most will find nothing. nothing but the remains of loved ones, skulls of children, sons and daughters who never had a shot at life. murdered by a state that cries the "right" to defend itself while its people enjoy lattes on sunny tel aviv patios and shopping trips on stolen land

ERAY SARIÇAM
But Were They All Naughty?
To the Poet of the Jewish Children of Warsaw
Variations on Oktay Rifat

1.
You never lay in a cradle,
Never slept in a swing,
Never even suckled –
You grew up to the sounds of phosphorus.

You held a slingshot in your hand,
Everyone you loved was gone.
Jews devoured your eyes –
No more seeing, no more crying.

You had a brother,
His body turned to ash.
He died, like all the others –
Now you are together.

He feels restless, misses the world,
Left his hands behind in Gaza,
Can't spin a hoop anymore.

2.
What happened to Leyan?
She went for water, came back thirsty.
She never got to wear a wedding dress,
Her tall, slender body – poof – vanished,
The crippled adorned themselves instead.

Leyan never savored life
Even as much as little Lili.
She never tasted salmon,
Never greeted
The birds that perched on her branches.
Never had a single moment

To bare her belly and be spoiled.

Leyan doesn't know she's dead.
They will take her out of the ambulance,
She cannot say, I won't leave.
She never tasted olives or dates.
Couldn't even say a word of thanks
To the agencies that made her voice heard.

3.
Leyan says, I was a child, too.
How was I any different from those in Warsaw?
We used to live in houses just like them.
Now, we are left outside every door.

Lies, she says, all poetry is lies.
We are not here,
We never were, Leyan says.

4.
Children who misbehave
Are locked away in hospitals,
Missiles are hurled at their heads,
They are hung by their hair on the walls.

But were they all naughty,
The children of Gaza?

ZULAL SEMA
Live Blog: Gaza – Non-intervention Principle*
Dedicated to the journalists who lost their lives in Gaza,

Friday, February 14, 2025

0000 GMT – for those who clench their fists around shards of glass,
it is time to open your palms
for all those drenched in blood,
this poetry is not poetry—
it is more than that
it will take the scar
it will give the scar
it is a جرّاحة —jarraha in Arabic,
a surgical operation upon the heart

0500 GMT—it is an operation upon all answers,
it is your trouble
thus, my tone is not for poetry lovers
my voice is for those
who must command the update
my voice is clear enough, clear enough to fight
Is writing poetry after Gaza also barbaric?
yes, these questions will be asked of me—
harsh and shattering
so that it is remembered
because I cannot borrow the question of silence
where words break off,
poetry begins
poems break at the edges,
gush out—
and then they exist

*Live blogging is a digital publishing format where updates are provided continuously, offering a real-time, chronological account of unfolding events

1300 GMT – romantic notions are slaughtered in the throat
I *"must live to tell your story"*
I smell jasmine from everyone, everywhere—
but now, it is not what I say
but what I will not say
that stands here
because dignity is forced to question itself
in the presence of the undignified
this is not the dignity of poetry –
this is Gaza's dignity
It is time to speak on behalf of justice,
live blog: Gaza – the center of pain

Monday, 7 October 2023

0900 GMT – this morning, like a scene from an old film,
the image grainy, caught between frequencies –
the radio crackles:
this news has belonged to every day since my childhood
breaking news: the West Bank, under Israeli occupation
In an abandoned rabbinical school,
I wake up as a captive,
my breath crackling, drowning in truths
sweat and sirens knot in my throat
I must move –
cutting through the crowd in Ramallah,
leaping over barriers,
before the last signal fades
because we are going live –
sharp as a shrapnel

Thursday, January 30, 2025

1714 GMT –The algorithm fragments truths
waiting to be spoken,
and 'Live Blog: Gaza' blurs into obscurity

In the newsroom,
words are weighed,
deemed too sensitive to breathe
a PRESS vest, soaked in blood –
one only grasps the scale of brutality
when someone close is lost
for this reason,
I refuse to wear a bulletproof vest inscribed with 'poet'
Instead, I will wear a silence heavier than headlines
because journalists are not merely reporters –
they are mourners in the heart of conflict

Monday, October 7, 2024

1500 GMT – a year of horrors no soul should endure
and everything shifted,
exactly a year ago,
since Saturday, October 7, 2023
Words falter, failing to capture war's devastation
We grasp for slogans:
"365 Days of Genocide,"
"Never Again,"
"War on Humanity," or "Genocide, Every Day" and Gaza...
the land of the most shattered bodies on Earth
here, a body carries as many wounds
as it can bear –
and more
In the newsroom, Gazan reporters
sometimes gaze into the distance,
their eyes adrift,
as collective trauma thickens the air

Sunday, January 19, 2025,

0710 GMT – In the cafeteria, my Gazan colleague,
Somaya Abueita,
softly hums "Rageen Ya Hawa"
She murmurs the lyrics,
"We are returning, my love"
Every ceasefire is fragile,
everyday births more death
But we will tell your story,
for each time, we hear the same refrain:
"We are not numbers"

Wednesday, January 22, 2025,

1530 GMT – I learned that the world can be merciless,
yes, we must begin by asking:
freedom, equality, justice – for whom?
for the voices buried beneath the rubble
for the hands grasping at fragments of yesterday?
because poetry rescues you before the knife reaches your throat –
it drags you from every dead-end street,
throws reality in your face,
and you –
you break it apart, piece by piece

1940 GMT – no gauze can stanch Gaza's wound
when blood becomes a dialect, people stir
eyes that refuse to close – a revolt
but to carry pain is not to rebury what's been seen
Palestine's heart beats beyond scalped words—
where language drowns in the raw salt of grief
to see is not enough
one must suture the skin of rubble

a Gazan boy before cameras: "No walls, only stones gnawing stones
... Even ash remembers the shape of home" "Where do you live now?"
"Half the house stands," he says, "the other half in my throat. I have
nothing but here."

Today,
Tuesday, January 28, 2025

1955 GMT – yesterday felt like a rehearsal
another Gazan colleague whispered:
"For the first time since the Nakba,
the idea of returning home feels real"
north or south,
the coordinates remain unchanged:
under occupation
yet, for the first time,
Palestinians are walking back –
toward historical Palestine
walk like
olive trees in motion –
rooted in return

CAO SHUI
The Shape of the Palestinian Son

The son of Palestine
Sleeping in a white shroud
In the shape of Palestine
His head is in the Sea of Galilee
This ancient harp is no longer able to make any sound
Along the Jordan River towards the Dead Sea
His heart is in Al Quds
This city of peace has been divided into two
The African Rift Valley splits open the entire planet
His little feet droop in the Gulf of Aqaba
This obstacle makes it impossible for him to stand
His blood flows down his legs
Dye the entire Red Sea.
The son of Palestine,
Please, wake up quickly,
Let's touch the shape of Palestinian land together

KADIR TEPE
The Sweater Woven from the Thread of the Sirat Bridge

our skin carved that fragile curse
we were a seesaw that broke its chain, oh Lord
a barren statue clung to the mind, the messenger's pocket torn
in the forest, the restless tree was chased, the hum of hives echoed in steps

the loudest flowers bloom in cemeteries, don't they?
mother, they kill children with small bullets, don't they?
a secret well sold – sin always searching for its inventor
fire paler than a shroud, melting, like raw dew distilled
the queen, perhaps, but bees sting once, then die once

does the stone feel pain when it skips on the river? do honor's veins crack?
on streets and in lobbies, silence holds the pulse of a nostalgic record
the room just now abandoned is the one that leaves home
death is the extra plate on the table, a slight stutter
our fate injected straight into our veins is plain, round as the earth
the wound fits best as clothing – wear blood as a belt
put on a sweater woven from the thread of the Sirat Bridge

so helplessness had hands and feet after all
the hive's hum clings to the glass of water handed out in war
a gun fired into the sea, the body washed back to its own shore

the loudest flowers bloom in cemeteries, don't they?
mother, they kill children with small bullets, don't they?
living was a narrow place
be careful—do the eyes you swallow belong to dead fish?

there was a rifle writhing, remembering the last poppy it aimed at
a blacksmith hammering his own finger, the hungry leaving the table
if the sun stays frozen in the sky, no fog can be worn
the boils forming in the whites of your eyes come from your weakness
how strange that a king's seal dirties a slave's shirt

red buds in a flowerpot, a wrong move in gambling, and the frog-princess
guess what lies behind the curtain—the breath of death, maybe
travelers wait on the platform, a grape on the vine is fed white wine
loneliness, patent leather shoes, cups, a windowsill, and a flattened land
the queen, perhaps, but bees sting once, then die once

it is beautiful, it is a bird, but it has bullet eyes, the messenger's pocket
   was torn
half an apple, a cigarette put out in the other half, a soup almost whole-
   almost gone
but what fell was only a leaf, blown towards the last trumpet

in the forest, the broken branch is the one being sought, front-page news
the siren, the cuffs, the police station—the mirrored room just abandoned
God will cut the mountains, hems always get soaked on mossy bridges
the earthquake was a mere itch on the eyelash

life ran along its long borders, tumors swelling in its empire
Palestinian children could have been our most beautiful scenery
mines could have been nothing but a sound effect
how shameful to buy the same blood thinner from a different store
between us and death, a lake—if a stone skips there, does it bleed?
the wind through the keyhole is a cherry stain no cloth can wipe away
or is it the blood on clashing swords in the sky that brings us the rain?

oh Lord, the seesaw without chains topples when it smiles
bees sting once, then die once
the bird hitting the glass—its mistake
death, like a sweater caught on the wires

if I sleep now, all songs will be sung in the same language
the loudest dead live in the world
mother, they kill children with small bullets, don't they?
living was a narrow place
was the curse broken?
please, remember...

KLARA VASSALLO
Running Order
after Lena Khalaf Tuffaha

there is a woman carrying the weight of her daughter at the shore
    of beit lahia,
wrapped in a sheet and, the first time, dips her into the sea
she realises that the sunlight reflects differently off the
    shattered glass of homes
she wants – wishes – to believe that she cannot perform acts
    for which no words exist.
when she looks at the sea and murmurs blue,
she wants to tell her indigo, but she wants to say gray, streaked with red.
and as she gazes at her veiled daughter,
she doubts the urgency of the red,
how it bursts forth from a white-clad body.
because there are no words to describe
the pain of red when you stare at it,
as she unties the shawl, removes her shoes and socks, loosens her hair,
a bracelet dangling from her wrist, matched to her own,
and everything is bathed in red.
she washes her in the rose-streaked water, wringing out fragments
    of her shirt,
and she wishes she could drift with her in this pale pink water,
to dream that dream one last time
; the one where fear seizes her lungs, and she stops breathing.
are you afraid of fear?
perhaps that is why there's nothing left outside on the streets, she says
because everyone is afraid.
and there is nothing
except phones ringing to warn of bombs falling on them,
and children dreaming of finding their mothers and tasting bread again.
and home is called by a name in a language
she barely understands anymore
and time she can no longer measure.
this woman wishes for her daughter,
to strip her of the name of her homeland,

to strip her to her bare skin,
and lay her naked in the sea to collide with a new country.
so that when she is rid of the fears of her home,
feeling every curve and hollow of her mother's body mirrored in her own,
this girl will not taste death.
as she sets her daughter afloat on the water's surface,
she lets the earth swallow her. she lingers there
her thighs heavy from days of fleeing to and from home,
clutching the remnants of her children.
she counts the freckles on their chests
the spots on their faces:
eighteen. nineteen. twenty. twenty-one. forty-five. fifty-nine.
one for every bomb that touches their ground.
and when she kisses her goodbye,
she hears another kiss descending onto her cheek from the sky
and no matter who she is. she shows them she is a woman. she shows them she can stand up.
and runs.

GRACIELA NOEMI VILLAVERDE
Gaza

Gaza, land of ancient olive trees,
its branches, arms that implore the sky,
its leaves, yellowish green tears,
under a scorching sun, a slow fire.

Its houses, boats stranded on the sand,
hit by waves of war and apathy,
its walls, stories engraved in stone,
of resistance and pain, an open wound.

Its children, flowers that grow among rubble,
with eyes that reflect an uncertain tomorrow,
full of the uncertainty of reconstruction.
its laughter, echoes that seek a tomorrow,
in a withered garden, with no spring nearby.

Its streets, rivers of tears and hope,
that flow among ruins, looking for a way out,
its people, stars that shine in the night,
despite the darkness, a light on.

Gaza, a poem written in blood and pain,
a song to life, which resists the clamor,
a cry of hope, which rises to the sky,
a call for peace, a new future.

MIRELA LEKA XHAVA
The Bell Tolls for You!
(Referring to the novel *For Whom the Bell Tolls*, 1940, Ernest Hemingway)

Fallen together in the same bed of war,
blood warms the snowy bedding, a fleeting moment.
Bubbles dance in the backdrop of Requiem War.
Two lives eternally frozen in spring,
sworn soldiers of "bunker" generals…

Eyes crossed without words.
The bullet killed speech,
lips kissed for the last time
a blood-stained rose,
upon the unsealed envelope of a letter
with no departure, no return…

For life, miles away, waiting until dawn.
The final gaze, tears and sky's thunder poured
over your meaningless funeral.
Daaang-daaang!
Hear it, so near – a mourning bell
by the Church. Someone will weep beneath a cypress,
while another, far from the burial path,
will rest "in peace" in his own soil –
the one called, without a name… Enemy!

Hear it as a curse and a cuckoo's lament,
an echo beyond the grave.
The bell tolls for you.

(Requiem War – Opus 66, Benjamin Britten)

ANNA YIN (CANADA)
Winter Solstice

If everything around seems dark,
look again, you may be the light
Rumi

The longest night descends,
its shadow wrapping the earth –
cold breath against each window,
while chill fingers stretch over bare trees,
for a moment,
the world disappears beneath a blanket of stillness.

Swirling, swirling...
a snowflake I become,
seeking a quiet glimmer,
small but steady,
waiting to be kindled –
 a single spark to melt the ice of despair,
to warm the coldest corners of this solstice night.

Look, stars are not far,
I inhale their stable rhythm,
the light within me rises,
growing brighter,
lifting me
toward another world.

Christmas Eve

Still so cold,
Still so silent.
The chimes of Christmas Eve will soon ring out,
Snow summits glisten with crystal light.
I recall the sunken wreckage at Pearl Harbor,
Names carved in silence on towering white walls.
I picture New York's dazzling lights,
Refugees fleeing at the Middle Eastern borders.
Prayers unceasing,
Suffering swelling like tides.
Christmas Eve, oh Christmas Eve,
The path to peace feels like a distant dream.
Still so cold,
Still so silent.
I long for songs long unheard,
I yearn for hearts of kindness.
Christmas Eve, oh Christmas Eve,
May peace no longer be absent from this world.

Shades of the Name

From The Diary of Anne Frank,
I remember few names, but long hiding days,
muffled silence, ghostly shades,
suppressed within walls.
At the age of fifteen, dates abruptly ended –
such a brief witness…
On the journey of Anna Karenina,
I foretell – a name was doomed.
Beauty, brain, and grace could not offset
the hierarchy of a husband's family name…
Name – a subject to fame
overshadowed saneness.
With Anne Boleyn's life,
I grasp the name as lost glory,
beheaded by power swings.
The victim, the sinner, and the witch…
all in one darkened the Tower of London.
Through Anna Akhmatova's voices,
I catch names exiled into deserts:
desert of despair, desert of cruelty, desert of humanity…
Names were pain, betrayers' baits,
dictators' game cards…
name misplaced in her beloved country.
Now, I choose "Anna" as my name –
an angel with a broken wing.
When darkness shrouds the sky,
I neither pray for God's mercy
nor ask for Mary's grace.
Instead, I seek poetry
as soaring wings.

First appeared in *Queen's Quarterly* in 2021

GHASSAN ZAQTAN
Oh River, Oh River

Take our people up north
help them with hunger, cold and wind
take the pictures of the dead and take their bread,
the travelers may starve.
Take their silence with them at dinners
when the birds sleep and ask for the keys.
Oh the river, oh, the river,
stay warm when their kids cross
smooth as silk
and continuing like commandments.
Graceful as a bridge does.

Black Horses

I want to save you like that song in elementary
which I carry whole with no errors
the tongue, tilted head, and the achiever.
The tiny feet stomping on the concrete floor with enthusiasm
and the open hands that knock on seats.
They all died in war, my friends and classmates.
And their tiny feet and excited hands remained,
knocking on the floors of rooms.
Tables, sidewalks, passers-by appearance and their shoulders.
And where I went
I hear her
and I see it.

The Dead in the Garden

Don't open the window
don't wake up
I beg you, don't wake up ...
they were dancing on the garden grass
as if they were the garden's motive
or its meditation
and they were screaming there

Beneath the light
their dust was coming apart

it had rained at night
all night.

Originally published in ***Like a Straw Bird It Follows Me****.*
New Haven: Yale University Press, 2012.

NOTES ON CONTRIBUTORS

Raed Anis Al-Jishi is a poet and translator from Qatif, Kingdom of Saudi Arabia. Al-Jishi, who has won international poetry awards., holds an honorary fellowship in writing from the University of Iowa, USA. He is one of the editors of *Contemporary Dialogues* from North Macedonia. His work has been translated into many languages.

Rıdvan Ardıç was born in Istanbul in 1990. He completed his studies in Cultural Management at Bilgi University. He has been actively involved in various literary associations and platforms and was part of the editorial team of Sözgelimi magazine. He was the first to translate the works of contemporary Russian poet Boris Ryzhy into Turkish. His poems and writings have been published in magazines and various fanzines. He has published three collections of poetry.

Lil Blume is a Jewish Canadian writer and teacher living in Hamilton, Ontario. She leads professional development workshops in empathic listening, conflict resolution, public speaking, effective teamwork, and communicating non-defensively. With the late poet, Ellen Jaffe, Lil organized three Hamilton Jewish literary festivals and published two anthologies to accompany the festivals: *From Sinai to the Shtetl and Beyond: Where is Home for the Jewish Writer?* and *Letters and Pictures from the Old Suitcase*. Lil's one-woman shows, *Every Marriage Is a Good Marriage – Even the Bad Ones* and *My Brain Tumour: A Comedy*, were presented at her 65th and 70th birthdays, respectively. She is currently writing a one-woman show for her 75th birthday, inshallah.

Taghrid Bou Merhi is a Lebanese-Brazilian poet, writer, journalist, editor, essayist, and translator fluent in multiple languages. She teaches Arabic to non-native speakers and works as a developmental trainer at the *Sawa Development Association*. She holds a law degree and serves as editor and head of translation for eight Arabic magazines. She also leads translation into Portuguese and Italian for *Translators Without Borders* and heads the translation department at *Azahar Poetic* magazine in Spain. In 2024, she was named among the *50 Most Influential Asian Women in Modern Literature* and one of the *Top 20 Global Journalists* by *Legacy Crown*. She has received numerous international awards. Her work has been translated into 48 languages. She has authored 23 books. Email: taghrid240@gmail.com

Hasan Bozdaş is a Turkish poet, writer and academic who was born in 1990. He has a Bachelor's degree in Law and a Master's degree in Human Rights Law. He worked as a lawyer for a while and followed the trials related to human rights violations. Currently a lecturer at Düzce University. Bozdaş works for various non-governmental organizations in the field of human rights and prepares reports. He is particularly interested in violations in Rohingya, Palestine and Syria. Bozdaş has two poetry books. *Adil Bir Akşam* was published by Hece Publications in 2018 and won the 2018 poetry award from the Association of Literature, Art and Culture Research (E.S.K.A.D.E.R). In 2023, his second book of poetry, *İnsanın Madde Olmayan Kısmı*, was published by Dergâh Publications. Bozdaş is the criticism editor of the poetry theory and criticism journal *Buzdokuz*.

Norbert Bugeja is an Associate Professor in Postcolonial Studies and Director of the Mediterranean Institute at the University of Malta. His poetry has been published in major international publications and read at poetry festivals worldwide. His collection *Oublie qu'elle n'est pas là* was published in France by Les Presses du Reél-Al Dante in 2023, in a translation by Irene Mangion, and appeared in Arabic from Editions Arabesques-Sheen in the same year. Bugeja was formerly a member of the International Advisory Council of the Anna Lindh Foundation, and General Editor of the *Journal of Mediterranean Studies*.

Tatev Chakhian, born in 1992 in Yerevan, is a Poland-based Armenian poet, translator, and visual artist. She pursued her education in Cultural Anthropology at Yerevan State University and later obtained a degree in International Relations and Border Studies at Adam Mickiewicz University in Poland. Chakhian's literary journey began with her debut poetry collection, *unIDentical*, in 2016. Her work reached a broader audience with its Polish publication *Dowód (Nie)osobisty* (I.K.M., 2018), nominated for the European Poet of Freedom Award in the same year. *Migrant Point* (Actual Art, 2024), her second poetry collection, offers a compelling exploration of the intricate layers of the migrant experience. Her poetry has been featured in over twenty languages worldwide. Chakhian translates and promotes Polish and Anglo-American poetry, bridging gaps between languages and cultures. *www.tatevchakhian.com*.

Franca Colozzo is an Italian Architect, writer, freelancer, blogger of U.N.S.D.G.s goals on Sustainability, poet, and former Italian teacher of "Design and History of Art" in Italy and Istanbul (Turkey) on behalf of the Ministry of Foreign Italian Affairs (M.A.E.). She was awarded four honorary doctorates. Recently, she was nominated "Executive Director" of the International Association: R.R.M.3 - RINASCIMENTO RENAISSANCE – MILLENIUM III, of which Prof. George Onsy (Egypt) is the founding President. Passionate about social justice, attentive to the rights of the weaker social classes and the importance of education for women and children, she currently deals with novels, poems, essays, and articles in various newspapers and blogs.

Lana Derkač is a prominent, award-winning poet and writer born in 1969 in Croatia. She graduated from the University of Zagreb, Faculty of Philosophy. Her publications include fifteen collections of poetry, short fiction, drama, essays, and a novel. Her individual pieces have been featured in numerous magazines, journals, and anthologies both in Croatia and abroad. Lana has received several important literary awards, including the Zdravko Pucak Poetry Prize, Duhovno Hrasce Prize, and Vinum et Poeta Prize, all of which were awarded in Croatia. Lana has participated in various literary events, both at home and abroad; her poems have been included in *Poetical Babylon* (a project by U.N.E.S.C.O. in Rome) and in *Rain of Poems above Dubrovnik* (a joint project between Chile and Croatia). Lana's work has been translated into 22 languages. Her latest publication is *Договор со правта* (Covenant with Dust), Skopje, 2024, poetry.

Josie Di Sciascio-Andrews has written seven collections of poetry: *The Whispers of Stones, Sea Glass, The Red Accordion, Letters from the Singularity, A Jar of Fireflies, Sunrise Over Lake Ontario and Meta Stasis*. Nature and one's place in it, as well as memory and social justice, are her muses. Her poems "The Red Accordion" and "Emerald City" were shortlisted for *Descant*'s Winston Collins Best Canadian Poem Prize and *The Malahat Review*'s Open Seasons Award, respectively. In 2015, her poem "Ghost" received first prize in the Big Pond Rumours Journal Contest. Josie is the author of two non-fiction books: *How the Italians Created Canada* and *In the Name of Hockey*. She is the host and coordinator of The Oakville Literary Cafe Series. Josie lives, teaches, and writes in Oakville, Ontario.

Leanne Ellul is a poet and prose writer who has published works for both adults and children. She was named Best Emerging Author in the 2016 Malta National Book Prize, and her work has won several awards. That same year, she was listed in the Commonwealth Young Achievers Book. Her poetry collections include *L-Inventarju tal-Kamra l-Kaħla* (2020), *Bjuda* (2022), and *Il-Manifest tas-Siġar* (2022). Her poetry has appeared in *adda, Asymptote, Modern Poetry in Translation, Columbia Journal*, and *Circumference*. Her works have been translated into Arabic, Croatian, Frisian, Italian, Greek, and Slovenian. In 2015, she published her first young adult novel, *Gramma*, followed by *be;n il-kmiem*. Both won Malta's Novels for Youth Literary Contest. Leanne lectures in Maltese literature and creative writing and is involved in N.G.O.s like Inizjamed and the H.E.L.A. Foundation. *www.leanneellul.net*.

Mar Fenech was born in Toronto to Maltese parents and spoke fluent Maltese before learning English. She is the author of *The Siege of Malta Trilogy*, a historical novel set in sixteenth-century Malta and *ürkiye*. Based on her trilogy, her award-winning television script, *Empires of Smoke*, is currently in development. She has also helped transform close to a hundred novels occupying shelves in bookstores worldwide as a top-rated, highly sought editor. Research has taken her to the ancient streets her characters roamed, the fortresses they defended, the seas they sailed, and the dungeons they escaped. Obstinate curiosity has led her to almost seventy countries across six continents. She does her best plot-weaving while hiking mountain trails, wandering local markets, paddle boarding cliff-sheltered bays, and lounging at home with her Siberian husky curled at her feet. For more information, visit https://marthesefenech.com

Abigail George is a South African novelist, screenwriter producer, essayist and poet nominated for the Pushcart Prize and is the 2023 winner of the Sol Plaatje European Union Poetry Prize, and shortlisted for the Writing Ukraine Prize. She is a Best of The Net-nominated essayist and poet who wrote for a symposium for a website based in Finland for a year. Her blog is called African Renaissance. She is the Contributing Editor for *African Writer Magazine* based in New Jersey, in the United States. Her essay "The Case Study of a Pelican (Insights from Hours in the Life of a Bipolar Girl)" was chosen as one of Afrocritik's 20 Remarkable African Essays for 2021. She writes about the human condition, and domestic relationships and believes writing can be both healing and therapeutic.

Joe Giampaolo was born in 1963 in Rome, Italy, and moved to Canada as a teenager. He studied philosophy at York University. He lives in Toronto with his family and their two dogs, Pixie and Buddy. Joe's publishing career includes thirteen books (essays, historical fiction and poetry) and countless newspaper and magazine articles in both Italian and English about poetry, politics, business and sports. Many of Joe's books have won literary awards and have been #1 bestsellers on Amazon in the U.S.A., the U.K., Canada, and Italy.

Elham Hamedi is an Iranian multimedia artist, painter, writer, and poet, and a dedicated executive member of several esteemed international associations and foundations. Her poetry collection *Un colpo alla testa era uno Zaqboor* (Terra d'Ulivi Editions, 2022) was published in Italy. Her artistic creations and literary works have been featured in numerous exhibitions, poetry anthologies, prestigious magazines, and renowned websites. Holding a Master's degree in Art and a Bachelor's degree in Radiology, Hamedi uniquely fuses her medical insights with artistic expression, exploring the intricate relationship between the human body and art through a psychoanalytic lens. Her participation in literary events has earned her numerous awards, underscoring her exceptional interdisciplinary creativity. Most recently, she was named one of the "50 Unforgettable Women of Asia" and recognized as a "Pillar of Asian Culture" as part of the global project Stockholm 2033—a five-volume initiative spanning five continents (2024).

Xanthi Hondrou-Hill is an award-winning Greek poetess who was born in Germany and studied German and English Literature, Linguistics, Journalism, and Public Relations Management in Germany. She has worked as a public relations manager at the Greek Consulate in Stuttgart and as a German, Greek, and English teacher. She is a professional translator. She has gained international recognition during the pandemic. Her poems have been published in many prestigious international media and anthologies around the world. In 2022, she won the first prize of the Gandhian Global Harmony Association, and in 2023, she earned the Rockport Poetry Festival Award. In 2023, she was awarded an honorary doctorate by C.I.E.S.A.R.T. in Madrid. She is the founder and director of the International Poetry Festival in Naoussa.

Jennifer Hosein is a Tiohtià:ke/Montreal-born writer, visual artist and educator of Trinidadian and South Asian ancestry residing in Tkaronto/Toronto. Her debut collection of poetry, *A Map of Rain Days*, published by Guernica Editions in 2020, was longlisted for the League of Canadian Poets 2021 Pat Lowther Memorial Award. Her poems, short fiction, creative non-fiction, and a play have been published in *The Fiddlehead*, *The Quarantine Review*, *Event*, *Rubicon*, *Makara*, and more as well as translated into Hungarian for the anthology *Crystal Garden/Kristálykert*. Her artwork has appeared on book covers, in magazines, and in solo and group exhibitions in Toronto; it is also featured on the cover of *A Map of Rain Days*. www.jenniferhosein.ca

Fady Joudah is a Palestinian American physician, poet, and translator who has published six collections of poetry. Joudah translated several collections of Palestinian poet Mahmoud Darwish's work in *The Butterfly's Burden* (2006), which won the Banipal Prize from the U.K. and was a finalist for the P.E.N. Award for Poetry in Translation, and *If I Were Another*, which won a P.E.N. U.S.A. award in 2010. His translation of Ghassan Zaqtan's *Like a Straw Bird It Follows Me* (2012) won the Griffin International Poetry Prize in 2013. He is the recipient of the Griffin Poetry Prize, The Arab American Book Award, and the Jackson Poetry Prize.

Rula Kahil is a poet and an assistant professor in the Sociology Department at the University of Toronto. Her journey into poetry emerged through her academic work, particularly during the writing of her Ph.D. dissertation on shame. Encouraged by her Ph.D. supervisor, Professor John P. Portelli, she began integrating poetry with her scholarship, recognizing its power as both an intellectual and emotional form of resistance. Since then, poetry has become the medium through which Rula expresses her passion for social justice, using it to explore themes of identity, displacement, and resilience. Originally from Lebanon, her lived experiences of occupation and war deeply inform her work, aligning with the struggles of the Palestinian people and other communities facing oppression. Through poetry, she resists injustice, challenges marginalization, and reclaims narratives often silenced by dominant discourse.

Zeynep Karaca was Born in 1988 in Ordu. She holds an associate degree in Theology and is currently a student in Public Administration at Istanbul University. She worked as an editor at Yeni Şafak newspaper for many years and produced content for G.Z.T. Yeni Medya. Currently, she works as an editor for the Karar newspaper. Her poems have been published in print magazines such as Şiir Versus, Buzdokuz, Akatalpa, Ruhsatsız, and Sadece Şiir, as well as online platforms like petroleus, Grunge Poetry, and Orlando. She has also published film articles in various magazines and online platforms.

Sheema Kalbasi is an Iranian-Danish-American humanitarian, researcher, poet, writer, and filmmaker whose work addresses feminism, war, refugees, human rights, and freedom of expression. A two-time Pushcart Prize nominee and nominee for the P.E.N. Award for Poetry in Translation, she has received a United Nations humanitarian award. Kalbasi has taught refugee children and worked with organizations such as the U.N.H.C.R., the Center for Refugees in Pakistan, and U.N.A. Denmark. In Denmark, she also trained and served as a defence soldier. Her poetry, translated into over twenty languages, has appeared in anthologies worldwide. Her poetry has been set to music for soprano and piano trio compositions. Notably, a composition based on her work was performed at the Smithsonian National Museum. She is the author of the poetry collection *Echoes in Exile* (P.R.A. Publishing, U.S.A., 2006), which was featured on Stony Brook University's Women and Gender Studies reading list. Her other works include *Spoon and Shrapnel: Verse and Wartime Recipes* (Daraja Press, Canada, 2024), *The Poetry of Iranian Women* (Editor, Reel Content Publishing, U.S.A., 2008), and *Seven Valleys of Love: A Bilingual Anthology of Women Poets from Medieval Persia to Present-Day Iran* (Translator, Editor, PRA Publishing, U.S.A., 2008).

Nibal Khalil is a Palestinian academic and a Professor of Anthropology who has a Ph.D. in Social and Cultural Anthropology from Charles University in Prague. She has held various academic and research roles at Charles University's Faculty of Philosophy and has consulted widely on gender issues, women's empowerment, and youth leadership, including her work with asylum services in Belgium. She served at Al-Quds University in Palestine as Dean of Scientific Research and as an advisor of the Higher Council for Youth and Sports in Palestine. Currently, Dr. Khalil is a Professor and Researcher at Birzeit University. Her research explores areas such as Bedouin communities, violence against women, and higher education systems. She has presented at various international institutions and led workshops across the United States, Europe, Egypt, Lebanon, Turkey, and Palestine. Dr. Khalil's contributions reflect her commitment to advancing understanding in anthropology and fostering academic dialogue on pressing social issues.

Yahia Lababidi is an Arab-American writer of Palestinian heritage and is the author, most recently, of *Palestine Wail* (Daraja Press, 2024) and *What Remains To Be Said* (Wild Goose Publications, 2025).

Milica Jeftimijević Lilić graduated from the Faculty of Philosophy in Pristina, earned a Master's degree in Philological Sciences at the University of Belgrade, and was a professor at the University of Pristina and a T.V. editor. She has published 33 books. Her poetry, prose, and essays have been translated into more than 30 languages. She is an academician of the Slavic Academy in Varna and has an honorary Doctor of Literature for the European Institute for Roma Studies. A literary critic, cultural activist, and promoter of world literature, she is a member of the Italian Council for Science and Law in Rome, which is part of U.N.E.S.C.O. She is living in Serbia.

Sonia Maddouri is a poet and editor from Tunisia. She has a degree in English literature. She has won several literary awards for her poetry in Tunisia, Iraq, Egypt, Sudan, and Italy. She has participated in many literary festivals in Morocco, Egypt, Algeria, Iraq, Saudi Arabia, Turkey, the U.A.E., Greece, Italy, and Iran. She has published five collections of poetry and a novel. Her poetry collection *The Pink Future Is Mine* (2017), won the Best Poetry Book award at the International Poetry Festival in Tozeur, Tunisia. She is a member of the Tunisian Writers Union.

Lisa Suhair Majaj is a Palestinian American writer. She is the author of *Geographies of Light* (winner of the 2008 Del Sol Press Poetry prize), two poetry chapbooks, two children's books, and poems and essays in journals and anthologies across the US, the Middle East, Europe, and India. She is also the author of literary criticism on Arab American literature and co-editor of three collections of essays on Arab and Arab American women writers, as well as of a forthcoming Companion to Arab American Literature. She has read at many international venues, including

Harvard's Center for Middle East Studies, London Southbank's Poetry International, Palestine Writes, World Social Forum (Tunisia), and World Court of Women against War for Peace (Bangalore, India). Her poems have been translated into Arabic, Greek, Hebrew, Malayalam, Spanish, German, and Lithuanian. She lives in Nicosia, Cyprus, 262 miles away from Gaza.

Marwan Makhoul is a Palestinian poet, born in 1979 in the village of al-Buqei'a, Upper Galilee, to a Palestinian father and a Lebanese mother. He works in engineering as a managing director of a construction company. He has several published works in poetry, prose, and drama, including the poetry collections *Hunter of Daffodils*, *Land of the Sad Passiflora*, *Verses the Poems Forgot with Me*, *Where Is My Mom*, and *A Letter from the Last Man*. For his first play, *This Isn't Noah's Ark*, Makhoul won the Best Playwright award at The Acre Theatre Festival in 2009. His poetry is also award-winning and has appeared worldwide in Arabic publications. Several of his poems have been set to music. Selections from his poetry have been translated into English, Turkish, Italian, German, French, Hebrew, Irish, Serbian, Hindi, Polish, Dutch, Albanian, Macedonian, Portuguese, Amharic, Eastern Armenian, Bangla, Hindi, Telugu, Tamil, Malayalam, Marathi, Russian, and Urdu. During the 2023 Gaza war, the following poem of his became a slogan raised by tens of millions of protestors and written on the walls of cities around the world: "In order for me to write poetry that isn't / political, I must listen to the birds / and in order to hear the birds / the warplanes must be silent." These lines became the world's loudest call for an end to the targeting of civilians.

Leila Marshy's father was exiled from Galilee in 1948, eventually landing in Canada; he was never able to return. During the First Intifada, Leila worked for the Palestinian Mental Health Association in Cairo and Gaza, and Medical Aid for Palestine in Montreal. In 2011, she founded Friends of Hutchison, a ground-breaking community group that brings Hasidic and non-Hasidic neighbours together in dialogue. She has published fiction and journalism in media in Canada and the US. Her first novel, *The Philistine,* was published in 2018 and published in France in 2021. She lives in Montreal.

Ahmed Miqdad is a Palestinian poet resident of Gaza. He has a B.A. in English and a Master's in Education. Ahmed is the author of three collections of poetry, *Gaza Narrates Poetry* (2014), *Stolen Lives* (2015), and *When Hope Is Not Enough* (2019), and a novel, *Falastin: The Hope of Tomorrow* (2018). He has witnessed over three wars and severe aggression by Israeli forces on the Palestinian people since the 1980s, with a huge loss of life. He writes and publishes to raise consciousness about the Palestinian cause. His latest collection is *The Shadow: Poems for Gaza* (October 2024), co-authored with John P. Portelli.

Maria Miraglia is a poet, essayist, translator, and peace activist. Her commitment to human rights and peace activism is evident in her long-standing memberships in Amnesty International, I.C.A.N., and the International Observatory for Human Rights. She is also the Vice President of the World Movement for the Defense of Children – Kenya and the founder of the World Peace Foundation. She is a founding member and Literary Director of the Pablo Neruda Association and a member of several editorial boards of international literary magazines. She is also a member of the International Writers Association and the International Academy Mihai Eminescu, an Honorary Member of the United Nations of Letters, a Poet Laureate of 2018, W.N.W.U,. and a World Poet Laureate, receiving the Golden Medal in 2020 in Xi' An, China. She received her most recent award, "50 Memorable European Women", from the Pontifical University Antonianum in Rome. Her poems have been translated into over thirty languages and are prominent in over one hundred anthologies worldwide.

Walid Nabhan is a Maltese writer, literary critic, and translator of Palestinian-Jordanian origin. He was born in Amman, Jordan to a family of refugees who had fled from their village home near Hebron Palestine during the 1948 Palestinian expulsion and flight. He has lived in Malta since 1990. He studied biomedical sciences at Bristol University and went on to obtain a Master's degree in Human Rights from the University of Malta. Nabhan has published three collections of short stories in Maltese, a collection of poetry, and two novels. The first novel, *Exodus of the Storks* (2013), won the Maltese National Prize for Literature in 2014 and the EU Prize for Literature in 2017. Nabhan has also translated several works of Maltese literature into Arabic.

Mirela Necula was born in the month of flowers, 1964, in Bucharest, Romania. She studied economics and has a degree in Accounting and Management Informatics. She is passionate about art, music, philosophy, and poetry. She has published 9 volumes of poetry, prose: *Love a Diamond in the Sadow* (Liric Graph Publishing), *Water lilies in the Eyes of Love* (Liric Graph Publishing), *My Love has Gone Around the earth* (Contratse Culturale), *Drunk and Guilty of Love* (Contratse Culturale), *Secret love* (Inspirescu Publishing House), *Trophy Heaven* (Inspirescu Publishing House), *Between Music and Eternity on a fine note* (Cervantes Publishing House), *Delilah with wings of fire* (Cervantes Publishing House), and *The rest is silence* (Cervantes Publishing House)

Mansour Noorbakhsh, writes poetry and fiction. His works have appeared in anthologies and journals including Verse Afire and WordCity (https://wordcitylit.ca). He has published three books, *In Search of Shared Wishes, Till You Recognize Me,* and *Powdery Wings*. Mansour is the York Region Branch Manager, a Member-at-Large on the Executive of The Ontario Poetry Society, and a member of The Writers' Union of Canada. In his writings, he tries to be a voice for freedom, human rights, and the environment. He presents The Contemporary Canadian Poets in a weekly Persian radio program (https://persianradio.net/poets/ or https://t.me/ottawaradio). Mansour Noorbakhsh is an Electrical Engineer. He lives with his wife and their two children in Toronto, Canada. Email: m.noorbakhsh@hotmail.com

Joseph C. Ogbonna is a prolific poet from Nigeria. Some of his works have been published very widely in journals, magazines, anthologies, and online blogs. His poems 'Napoleon to Josephine and Josephine to Napoleon' were aired by B.B.C. Radio 3 for the bicentenary of the death of Napoleon Bonaparte on May the 21st, 2021. He is also an Amazon International best-selling co-author. He was a high school teacher at a British International Private School, where he taught history. He lives in Enugu, Nigeria.

Muhammed Hüseyin Özer was born in 1996 in Ağrı, Turkey. He earned his undergraduate degrees in Classroom Teaching from Mersin University and in Sociology from Anadolu University. He later pursued a Master's degree in Classroom Teaching Education at Mersin University. His poems and articles have been published in numerous literary and academic journals. He serves as the editor of Telmih Kültür Sanat Tarih ve Edebiyat Dergisi and Telmih Kitap. He is also the author of the poetry book *Fel*. Currently, he works as a project coordinator at the Ministry of National Education and resides in Istanbul.

Gianna Patriarca is a multiple award-winning author of 13 books, poetry, children's literature, short fiction, and essays. Her work has been adapted for Canada Stage Theater, C.B.C. radio drama, and is the subject of numerous documentaries. Her work is extensively anthologized and appears on the course list of universities in Canada, the U.S.A., and Italy. Her first collection, *Italian Women and Other Tragedies* is in its 4th printing has been translated into Italian. *This Way Home*, a collection of selected and new work, won the Pier Giorgio Di Cicco Poetry Prize 2024. She was the first recipient of the Arts and Science Award from the Italian Chamber of Commerce. Gianna is working on a new collection of poems, *Just Go*, a novel, *The Sicilian's Bride,* and story books for children. She lives in Toronto.

John P. Portelli, originally from Malta, is a professor emeritus in the Department of Social Justice Education at the University of Toronto. He has taught in Canadian universities since 1982. Besides 11 academic books, he has published ten collections of poetry (four in Maltese and English, one in English and French, three in Maltese, one in English (*Here Was*, available from Amazon), and one in Greek, *The Loves of yesterday*), two collections of short stories (one translated into English and published as *Everyday Encounters*), and a novel, *Everyone but Faiza* (Burlington, O.N.: Word and Deed, 2021). His literary work has been translated into Italian, Romanian, Greek, Farsi, Arabic, Korean, English, Spanish, Portuguese, and Polish. His latest collection, *Here Was* has been translated and published in Romanian in June 2023, in Arabic in November 2023, in Italian in January 2024, in Farsi in February 2024, and in Turkish in May 2024. *Here* was was short-listed for the Canadian Book Club Award in October 2024. Five of his books have been short-listed for the Malta Book Council Annual Literary Award. He now lives between Toronto and Malta and beyond! His latest collection is *The Shadow: Poems for Gaza* (October 2024), co-authored with Ahmed Miqdad.

Niloy Rafiq, from Maheshkhali, Cox's Bazar, Bangladesh, has been writing in the literary pages of local daily newspapers since his school days. Later, his poems were published in national and international literary magazines. His poems have been translated into more than twenty languages. He has published six collections of poetry in Bengali, and two collections in English.

Shirani Rajapakse is an internationally published, award-winning poet and short story writer from Sri Lanka. She has won the *Ossi di Sepia Award in* Italy, the *Kindle Book Award for Poetry*, U.S.A., and *The Boao International Poetry Award in* China, and is a thrice recipient of the *State Literary Awards for Short Stories* Sri Lanka in addition to numerous other awards. Rajapakse's work appears in many journals and anthologies around the world including in *Dove Tales, Buddhist Poetry, Litro, Linnet's Wings, Bosphorus Review, Berfrois, Harbinger Asylum, Flash Fiction International, Voices Israel, Silver Birch, About Place, Poetry Lab Shanghai, Mascara* and more, and has also been translated into Spanish, Farsi, Urdu, Hindi, Chinese and French. Rajapakse read for a B.A. in English Literature from the University of Kelaniya, Sri Lanka and has an M.A. in International Relations from J.N.U., India. *www.shiranirajapakse.wordpress.com*

Giovanna Riccio is a prize-winning poet, book reviewer, sometimes-lecturer, and teacher who thrives on intellectual pursuits; she is graduate of the University of Toronto where she majored in philosophy. She is the author of *Vittorio* (Lyricalmyrical Press, 2010) *Strong Bread* (Quattro Books, 2011), and *Plastic's Republic* (Guernica Editions, 2019) which was a finalist for the 2022 Bressani Prize. Her work has appeared in national and international publications, numerous anthologies and has been translated into six languages. Her most recent lecture is titled "Barbie as a Work of Art: Barbie meets Walter Benjamin." Website and contact: www.giovannariccio.com.

Omar Sabbagh is a very widely published poet, writer, and critic from the UK and Lebanon. His poetry and prose have appeared in many prestigious venues. *For Echo* is his sixth poetry collection with Cinnamon Press, released in Spring 2024. He has published two novellas and much short fiction, too, some of it prize-winning. *Y Knots: Short Fictions* was published in 2023 with Liquorice Fish Books. His latest work, *Night Settles Upon the City,* a collection of poetry out of contemporary Beirut, is published with Daraja Press, in November 2024. He holds a Ph.D. in

English Literature from K.C.L. He has taught in several Universities. Currently, he teaches at the Lebanese American University (L.A.U.).

Paul Salvatori *is a Toronto-based journalist, community worker, and artist. He earned a doctorate in philosophy from the University of Ottawa.* He has been proactive in social justice initiatives. This includes working with marginalized populations, mentorship and outreach, facilitating youth programs, peer support, art, journalism, and group advocacy. Prior to this, he was an educator at various academic levels—university, junior college, etc.—offering and designing courses in ethics, social science and cultural studies. "Passionate as I am as an educator, I have over the years been drawn, as it were, away from the classroom and more directly into the realm of community work." *Much of his work on Palestine involves public education, such as through his recently created interview series, "Palestine in Perspective" (The Dark Room Podcast), where he speaks with writers, scholars, and activists.*

Eray Saricam was born in 1993 in Gebze. His poems and writings have been published in various literary magazines, including Karabatak, Fayrap, İtibar, Hece, Şiir Versus, Ruhsatsız, Olağan Şiir, Söğüt, Muhit, Aşkar, Kayıp Kayıt, Bir Nokta, Cins, Lacivert, and Sabit Fikir. He has published three collections of poetry and two collections of literary criticism.

Zulal Sema is an Istanbul-based poet, journalist, and literary critic of Meskhetian Turkish origin. She holds a degree in Political Science and International Relations. Her poetry draws strength from the epic emphasis of lyrical narrative, aiming to create cinematic scenes within her poems. Her work has been published in various literary magazines, including *Itibar and Muhit*. In 2020, she published her debut poetry collection, *Kendi Sesinden (Own Voices)*. Zulal actively contributes to the literary community by organising poetry workshops and participating in literary talks and panels. As a journalist at TRT World, she highlights Turkish-based artists, exploring their lives, creative journeys, and social impact. She is passionate about creative writing and its influence on society.

Cao Shui is a Chinese poet, novelist, screenwriter, and translator. He is a representative figure of Chinese Contemporary Literature. He leads the Great Poetry Movement. His most notable works include *Epic of Eurasia* and *King Peacock* (T.V. series). He is the author of forty books, including ten poem collections, five essay collections, ten novels, four translations, eighteen fairy tales, and one hundred episodes for T.V. series and films. He has won more than 50 literary awards worldwide. His works have been translated into 24 languages. He is also chief editor of Great Poetry, deputy editor in chief of World Poetry, Asian coordinator of World Poetry Movement, secretary general of Boao International Poetry Festival, and vice president of the Silk Road International Poetry Festival. Currently, he lives in Beijing.

Kadir Tepe was born in 2001 in Istanbul. He is currently pursuing a degree in Turkish Language and Literature at Marmara University. His work spans various literary genres, including poetry, short stories, essays, criticism, and interviews. He has published five collections of poetry. His work has been published in magazines such as Buzdokuz, Söğüt, Hece, Edebiyat Ortamı, Türk Edebiyatı, Cins, Nihayet, Olağan Şiir, Kayıp Kayıt, Sadece Şiir, Akatalpa, KafagözSanat, Ayarsız, and Okur, as well as on various online platforms. His poetry has been translated into multiple languages. Alongside M. Burak Çelik, he co-publishes Ruhsatsız Dergi and serves as the editor of the Fabrik Kitap-Ruhsatsızşiir series. He writes poetry critiques for the online platform Kitaphaber and hosts the digital literary program Bibliyofil. Additionally, he organizes various literary events and works as a copywriter/chief editor at a public institution.

Klara Vassallo fell in love with the arts as a child. In 2024, she graduated with a Bachelor of Arts (Hons.) in Maltese from the University of Malta and is currently researching the potential of poetic language for huma suffering for her Master of Arts in Maltese Literature. Klara writes and performs poetry in both Maltese and English and has achieved recognition by placing first in the Doreen Micallef National Poetry Contest. In 2022, she published her first chapbook, ħoss ħsejjes — a collection of prose poetry that explores the sounds of her childhood and how these resonate with and out of her as a woman. Additionally, Klara has theatrical arts at heart, enriching her creative expressions with a profound love for the stage and all that happens around and off it.

Graciela Noemi Villaverde is a writer and poet from Concepción del Uruguay (Entre Rios) Argentina, based in Buenos Aires. She graduated in letters and is the author of seven books of poetry, which have won several awards. She works as the World Manager of Educational and Social Projects of the Hispanic World Union of Writers and is the U.H.E. World Honorary President of the same institution, Activa de la Sade, Argentine Society of Writers. She is the Commissioner of Honor in the executive cabinet in the Educational and Social Relations Division of the U.N.A.C.C.C. South America Chapter.

Mirela Leka Xhava is a Franco-Albanian poet who graduated in Albanian Language and Literature at Aleksander Xhuvani Elbasan University. Until 2002, before immigrating to France, she worked as a librarian. Her poems have been published in prestigious magazines, newspapers and anthologies internationally. She is active in literary salons and fairs in France, as well as contemporary literature, where she won the "Diplôme d'Honneur at the 24th Printemps des Poètes.
-Sartrouville France". She has recently been accepted as a member of the Association of French Poets. She has published four collections of poetry, her latest *Au-delà de moi-même*, Editions Maïa Paris 2025

Anna Yin was Mississauga's Inaugural Poet Laureate (2015-2017) and has authored six poetry collections and four books of translations including *Mirrors and Windows* (Guernica Editions). Her poems/translations won awards and appeared at A.R.C. Poetry, New York Times, Queen's Quarterly, China Daily, C.B.C. Radio etc. She teaches Poetry Alive, and her 11th book will be published by Frontenac Press in 2025.

Ghassan Zaqtan Born near Bethlehem, Palestinian poet, novelist, and editor Ghassan Zaqtan has lived in Jordan, Syria, Lebanon, and Tunisia. A poet who writes primarily in Arabic, Zaqtan is the author of numerous collections of poetry, including *The Silence That Remains: Selected Poems* (2017) and *Like a Straw Bird It Follows Me* (2012), both translated by Fady Joudah; *Ordering Descriptions: Selected Poems* (1998); and *Early Morning* (1980). *Like a Straw Bird, It Follows Me* won the 2013 Griffin Poetry Prize. Zaqtan is also the author of the novels *Old Carriage with Curtains* (2011) and *Describing the Past* (1995), among others, and the play *The Narrow Sea*, which was honoured at the 1994 Cairo Festival. A supporter of the Palestinian resistance movement, Zaqtan has edited the

Palestine Liberation Organization's literary magazine, *Bayader*, as well as the poetry journal *Al-Soua'ra* and the literary page of the Ramallah newspaper *Al-Ayyam*. Founding director of the House of Poetry in the West Bank city of Ramallah, Zaqtan has also served as director general of the Palestinian Ministry of Culture's Literature and Publishing Department. He lives in Ramallah.

ALSO FROM DARAJA PRESS

Night Settles Upon the City
Omar Sabbagh

Written with urgency out of a war-time Beirut, this poetry collection registers the griefs and the heroism of the Lebanese, under siege yet again. Sabbagh lends his lyrical voice here, trying to find some harmonic sense out of catastrophe.

While much of the work was written swiftly, on impulse, and almost like, as one of the poem's title's has it, a 'War Diary,' in verse, this work aims nonetheless to last in its significance and resonance at a time when the world as a whole (let alone Lebanon herself) has become so unpredictable, so fickle and so perilous.

ISBN 978-1-998309-33-7 • $16

Palestine Wail
Yahia Lababidi

Palestine is personal for writer Yahia Lababidi. His Palestinian grandmother, Rabiha Dajani — educator, activist & social worker — was forced to flee her ancestral home in Jerusalem, at gunpoint, some eighty years ago.

As an Arab-American, Lababidi feels deeply betrayed by the USA's blind support of Israel's genocide of Palestinians.

In *Palestine Wail*, Lababidi reminds us that religion is not politics, Judaism is not Zionism, and to criticize the immoral, illegal actions of Israel is not antisemitism.

ISBN 978-1-998309-11-5 • $18

Prices in U.S. dollars · www.darajapress.com

www.ingramcontent.com/pod-product-compliance
Lightning Source LLC
Chambersburg PA
CBHW070937180426
43192CB00039B/2310